If you care about others it is not enough to try to provide food banks, and to complain when government and others' action or inaction impoverishes the population. You also have to be concerned with what everyone needs – which is a home. All our lives are harmed when others find it so hard to be safely housed. We need to question why rents are so high, why house prices are so high, and why respect and love for our neighbours appears has fallen so low.

Professor Danny Dorling
Chair of Human Geography, Oxford University

Good housing is one of the foundations of good society. Poor housing damages health, limits the potential of young people and robs hope from those who have to live in it. This book is an important contribution to the debate about the future of housing and how we should be building to make lives better across the country for this and for future generations. Across Scotland, across the UK and across the world we have to be building a better tomorrow for the generations that follow us and decent housing has to be part of the foundations of that.

Deidre Brock
MP, Edinburgh North and Leith

Always honest, sometimes blunt, always thoughtful, sometimes challenging, these well-informed yet ultimately hopeful essays are a challenge to society to face some home truths and a challenge to the church to translate the worthy theology of heavenly believing into the practical ethics of earthly belonging.

Rev Dr Sam Wells
vicar, St Martin-in-the-Fields, London

Thirty years ago, I recall writing an essay in which I argued that one of the litmus tests of the morality of a nation was the extent to which there was accessible and affordable housing for everyone. On that basis, the UK has become dramatically less moral since the 1980s. *Foxes Have Holes* is a timely and enlightening read, laying out a superb historical and contemporary analysis of the housing movement. It sets out why Christians, alongside others, must be committed to bringing about change and it articulates what needs to change and why. Above all, this book on housing is not about bricks and mortar but about a commitment to human flourishing. Read it and you will want to change things.

Martin Johnstone
Secretary of the Church of Scotland's Church & Society Council;
he lives in a Glasgow tenement

Our country doesn't face a single housing crisis, but multiple crises of affordability, availability, sustainability and suitability. Having a 'home' is central to our development and fulfilment as human beings, and therefore to the health of our communities. This collection of essays is a timely reminder of why we are where we are, and is a challenge to action for people of faith.

Rachel Lampard
vice-president elect, Methodist Conference

Through working with networks supporting asylum seekers and refugees in finding accommodation, we know just how crucial decent, safe housing is – not least for people living at the edge. The priority of affordable homes for all lies at the heart of this book. I welcome its timely challenge to churches and politicians to invest in a livable future.

Pat Bennett
programme development worker, Iona Community

Foxes Have Holes ... is such an important document. The problem can't be solved without intervention. To solve the housing crisis, you have to face up to a political crisis.

Frank Cottrell Boyce
screenwriter, novelist and actor

Foxes Have Holes

FOXES HAVE HOLES

CHRISTIAN REFLECTIONS ON BRITAIN'S HOUSING NEED

EDITED BY
ANDREW FRANCIS

Ekklesia

First published in 2016

Ekklesia
235 Shaftesbury Avenue
London
WC2H 8EP
www.ekklesia.co.uk

The views expressed by individual contributors to this volume are not necessarily those of Ekklesia.

Production: Bob Carling (www.carling.org.uk)
Cover photograph: Martin Atkinson
Managing Editor: Simon Barrow
Business: Virginia Moffatt, Henrietta Cullinan

ISBN: 978-0-9932942-2-8

A Catalogue record for this book is available from the British Library.

Contents

Preface

For the second title in Ekklesia's new book imprint, focusing on trans-
formational possibilities in church and society, we are delighted to be
publishing this important multi-author volume looking at a different
future for housing in Britain. We are grateful to all the contributors,
to editor Andrew Francis, to Alison Gelder of Housing Justice, and to
everyone who has supported and enabled this project.

Though the subtitle of *Foxes Have Holes* points specifically to
Christian responses to housing need (and, indeed, what many are
necessarily describing as a housing crisis in Britain today), that term
'Christian' should not be read in an exclusive or back-slapping way.
On the contrary, as the book you are reading amply demonstrates,
Christians can and should be working with those of other faiths and
no religious belief (people of 'good faith', one and all) to address these
issues adequately – starting with the particular insights we have to offer from our different places of engagement.

Those locations include the different nations and regions of Britain.
The contexts of England, Scotland and Wales offer different perspectives and resources for addressing housing need. Power, we believe,
needs to be brought as close as possible to the people it impacts.
Subsidiarity and self-determination in the context of partnership
across recognised local, regional, national, cultural and social bound-
aries is vital. So the issues and ideas raised by the contributors to
Foxes Have Holes can be learned from, and applied, in a variety of ways
across these islands.

In policy terms, four principles are key to genuinely transforma-
tional change from Ekklesia's viewpoint. First, nurturing the belief that
a better future is possible through cooperation and mutuality. Second,
the conviction that the moral and practical worth of any policy should
be judged by its impact on the most excluded, marginalised and vulnerable. Third, a commitment to struggle for policy alternatives that
arise from the experience and knowledge of those living at the sharp
end of how power is currently (mis)used. Fourth, supporting change
from the ground up rather than the top down.

All those values are reflected in this book. They also tie in directly
with a vision of twenty-first-century Christianity that is about empow-
erment not hierarchy, liberation not domination, and freedom not co-
ercion. In a just society everyone deserves and needs a decent home

and the security that makes this possible. That is the commitment and vision behind this book.

Simon Barrow
Co-director, Ekklesia

The title of this book

A word about the title may be necessary for those unfamiliar or less familiar with the biblical background to the term. The main phrase comes from a saying of Jesus recorded in both the Gospel of Luke and the Gospel of Matthew. In Matthew 8:20 Jesus is depicted as responding to a rabbi (teacher) who declares an intention to follow him loyally. He replies: 'Foxes have holes and birds of the air have nests, but the Son of Man has no place to lay his head.'

The terminology has several references. Jesus, who for Christians is the human one in whom God fully dwells, declares himself to be without permanent abode – he is on a mission, and is operating as an itinerant teacher, healer and prophet. The curious phrase 'Son of Man' is a reference back to the kingship tradition of Ancient Israel. Yet Jesus is no ruler and has no palace. He mixes with, and advocates for, ordinary people, not least the excluded and marginalised.

The Greek word translated 'son' (*huios*) is used elsewhere in the New Testament to denote a loving servant, an attendant, a guest, one of 'the masses' and a subject of the powers that be. Here Jesus is directly identifying with working people, including those pushed off the land. To follow him is to embark on a journey of solidarity.

There is also a link to the powerful passage at the end of Matthew's Gospel where those who claim to be God's people are challenged with the reminder and warning, 'I was homeless and you offered me no welcome' (25:43). Housing the neighbour and the stranger are firm obligations for followers of Jesus.

Foreword

As I write a few days before Homeless Sunday 2016, there is no argument that housing is one of the key issues on the political agenda and will be the top priority for the candidates in May's London mayoral election. So this polemic for better housing for all and call for church and Christian involvement could not be better timed.

Housing Justice, the charity I lead, stands in a tradition of Christian housing activism, building on the work of *Faith in the City* (the main author of the housing chapter was our first Chief Executive, Robina Rafferty). In my work there I spend about half of my time speaking up for current church action on housing and homelessness and advocating for better solutions for people experiencing homelessness and housing need – and the other half inspiring and encouraging churches to do more, and equipping them to provide more and better solutions through training, toolkits and other support.

There is undoubtedly a need for more discussion and reflection – but also for more and better information. When I speak to church audiences the first thing I encourage them to do is to share any experience they have about homelessness and housing need – because, as Andrew Francis rightly points out, housing is not a problem for the majority of the population. Folk who are outright owners, or have had a mortgage for a while, or who are secure council or housing association tenants, are not generally struggling with high housing costs, disrepair or overcrowding; for them housing is not a problem. So it is vital that those of us who do have stories of difficulty, privation and insecurity don't keep them to ourselves.

The second thing I ask people to do is to research housing in their area. There is a wealth of information about everything from homelessness and housing need to rents and house prices as well as indices of deprivation and strategies for moving forward from local authorities, government statistics and online vendors like Zoopla. Too often we assume that our own situation is the norm and build our reflection and action upon that shaky foundation. So I encourage you to follow up the references in the footnotes, to research the situation in your own community and to share your housing story.

It is important too to keep reiterating the fact that Britain is not in danger of being concreted over if more homes are built. In reality only around 10 per cent of the land is built up in any way (this includes all so-called brown field sites) and all the housing we have at the moment covers less than 2 per cent of the land, so that even if the green field land used for housing was doubled it would scarcely be noticeable. And that is without starting on work to use the empty roofs of low-rise shops and offices where one or two floors of flats could easily be added.

Another key point that is frequently overlooked but is well spelled out in the chapters that follow is that the market has never provided adequate housing for people at the bottom of the social ladder. One of the good points about UK housing noted by the UN Rapporteur in 2014 was that, thanks to the investment in social housing in the twentieth century, the experience of poverty in Britain does not, as in most countries, go hand in hand with poor housing.

Some of the language that is used about housing tends to obscure rather than reveal the true situation. For example, the government has taken the word 'affordable' and is using it to describe a wide range of types (and prices) of housing. Affordable housing in the context of the Housing and Planning Bill 2015–16 (and previous Coalition legislation) now includes homes let by housing associations at up to 80 per cent of market rents, shared ownership homes and subsidised homes to buy, such as starter homes. Affordability is defined in terms of the house-building, house-buying and private-rental sector markets. It does not mean what most people would suppose – that the people accessing the homes can pay the rent (or mortgage) and still have enough left to cover food, fuel and the other necessities of life. So there is significant work to do on the information and education front if we are to strive for a fresh national political consensus about housing as urged in the final chapter.

One of the barriers to coordinated church action – and reflection – on housing is the fact that housing is a devolved matter and over the last fifteen years housing policy in Wales and Scotland has gradually moved further away from England. The Housing and Planning Bill 2015–16, which is currently making its way through the parliamentary process, will have a profound effect on housing in England and increase the distance between the three nations. As with the Welfare Reform and Work Bill 2015–16, much of the serious opposition is likely to come in the House of Lords and many of the details of the law are to be found in yet-to-be-published regulations and not on the face of the Bill. There are many aspects of concern in the Bill but perhaps the most disturbing in the context of this book is the absence of any recognition of what makes a housing unit a home. There is complete invisibility of the factors that need to be in place for the people who live in the houses we plan and build to form them into homes. In responding to the call to action with which this volume ends the churches must be ready to go back to basics in reflecting among themselves and with wider civil society about the human need for adequate shelter and the meaning of 'home'.

It feels appropriate at this point to share my own housing story. I was brought up in a succession of detached houses (my father, having grown up over a shop in an inner-city, terraced high street, had a thing about 'detached'), mainly in northern England, which my parents were buying with a mortgage. At university and in my twenties, like a lot of people, I shared flats and houses, sometimes with people I knew and sometimes with strangers. During this time, I also had a spell of hidden homelessness when a relationship ended and I had to move out of the flat I was sharing at short notice, staying on friends' floors and sofas while I flat-hunted and saved for a deposit. Once married I became a mortgage payer and later a landlord and a tenant again because I had to move my family temporarily to Cambridge in order to study there. And now that my children are adults and have formed their own households, my husband and I have downsized to a maisonette on a council estate which we own outright as leaseholders. This last property is the first one we have chosen specifically as a long-term home and I am happy to be putting down roots in the rooms and in the community.

Before we made this move I took a sabbatical from my work at Housing Justice and we lived out of (fairly small) rucksacks for four months while we walked, backpacking, from Walsingham in North Norfolk through France to Santiago de Compostela in Northern Spain. We reflected a lot about home and homelessness as we walked and one of the conclusions that came to me was that for me, home is where my husband, Ian, and I are together. It is a virtual space that we carry with us and create each night as we prepare food to eat and carry out other domestic tasks like washing clothes. So for me 'home' is not tied to a building, notwithstanding my home-ownership. The question I am still working on is how to witness to this lack of attachment while also being committed to the community on my estate and to offering hospitality.

Alison Gelder
Chief Executive, Housing Justice

Introduction

Andrew Francis and Trisha Dale

'How the great housing disaster defines our times and what we can do about it?' is the subtitle of Danny Dorling's 2014 book on UK housing.[1] Dorling is the Halford Mackinder Professor of Geography at Oxford University, but more importantly a highly respected and influential commentator about social inequalities in modern Britain. No matter how we vote, there is a huge problem about Britain's housing. The urgency of the problem is reflected in the language used to express it – disaster, crisis – but everyone agrees that people in Britain need adequate housing.

This book is an unashamed polemic for better housing for all. That will mean both numerically more and a diversity of homes – at affordable prices.

In the autumn of 2015, all the six major British political parties mentioned Britain's housing need, to greater and lesser extent, within speeches on other subjects. On 14 October 2015, *The Times* and several other quality newspapers brought together housing reports and government documentation declaring that, because of inward net UK migration, during the next decade, 'three more cities of the size of Birmingham' will be needed to accommodate everyone. All this comes against the background of a growing indigenous population, with increasing numbers of elderly people and, in some neighbourhoods, single-person households.

However, there is little political consensus about how Britain's housing need is to be met, alongside the employment/unemployment, welfare payment and healthcare issues involved. By Christmas 2015, the right-of-centre parties favoured increasing right-to-buy options whereas left-of-centre parties favoured increasing the stability of an affordable rental sector. The big questions cannot easily nor quickly be resolved; therefore housing will be a major, recurring political issue for at least the next decade.

Mediating yet prophetically challenging voices are needed. Christians and the churches to which they belong, as well as other faith communities, can offer such voices and practical insights into the necessary debate to encourage creative solutions for the whole nation. This book seeks to provide insights into and information for such discussions, which must take place at every level of our communities from neighbourhood to nation. Inevitably, it is published at a moment in time; the cut-off point for the chapter contributors was 30 November 2015. Further developments are occurring!

The writers speak as followers of Jesus. We are an ecumenical and diverse group. Our words are each our own, and do not automatically reflect the ongoing social and theological commentary which Ekklesia, the Christian think-tank, as this book's publisher, will develop as the housing debate continues.

That debate does not continue in isolation. Housing needs are integrally bound with matters of funding. *The Independent* reported that:

> Britain's estimated £25bn housing benefit bill for 2015–16 is being fuelled by soaring rents in the most prosperous part of the country as workers struggle to find affordable accommodation . . . Welfare spending is growing rapidly in the boom areas of South-east of England, largely driven by the growing cost of housing benefit payments, according to the Centre for Cities think-tank.[2]

The need for welfare reform, built around Jesus' values for the oppressed, marginalised and homeless (rather than economic self-centredness), is apparent in these pages, but here we focus upon the housing crisis.

So this book begins with the Bishop of Manchester's chapter on what makes a home. Bishop David's ministry is renowned for his advocacy on behalf of the homeless, and his work in leading housing initiatives for marginalised people. Chapter 2, by Andrew Francis, who is a community theologian, explores the history of Britain's housing provision.

The majority of this book is written by housing experts, each from their own professional field's perspective as well as that of their diverse, passionate Christian discipleship. In Chapter 3, Sean Gardiner explores the changing role of local authority provision while, in Chapter 4, Chris Horton examines the complementary role of housing associations. Helen Roe, a London-based architect, looks at current flagship projects in London's cityscape in Chapter 5, and explains why so much thinking about housing is London-centric. Then, in Chapter 6, Helen Woolley helps us re-examine the reasons why 'open space' factors must form part of any answers which take 'quality of life' seriously. In Chapter 7, Raymond Young offers a distinctive contribution about the role of communities and rural solutions to the wider discussion, highlighting Scotland's rich interplay between meeting both urban and rural needs. Then, in Chapter 8, Paul Lusk, a planning consultant and community-enabler, challenges us critically to look 'beyond welfare housing'.

In Chapter 9, Andrew Francis draws together some of the cohering theological strands to help all readers continue constructing their own theology of housing. Finally, we offer ten 'Action Points' which can provide issues and questions for local debate as well as prompts for strategic, practical action.

Chapter One

A Sense of Belonging

David Walker

At the heart of the Christian message lies an invitation to belong. Or perhaps it's an invitation to recognise that we already belong. We belong with the one in whose image we are made; the one who is both our origin and our final destiny. We believe that the God with whom we belong has sealed that belonging in the events of the life, death and resurrection of Jesus Christ. Through the Holy Spirit, God has made a home within us, a foretaste of the eternal home we shall have in God. Yet Christian belonging goes beyond the internal and spiritual life. We belong through and with the routines of our lives, the special events we mark out, the people we have around us and the places with which we identify. We are invited to immerse ourselves in these belongings, and to be the means by which others, whether they share our faith or not, are afforded a rich experience of human belonging too.

For me, this is where the imperative for Christians to engage in questions of housing emerges. What are the things that you and I must have, by way of housing, if we are to be able to feel that we truly belong? What are the factors in Britain's housing situation today, and across the wider world, that enable or inhibit human belonging? And what can we do to impact upon them for good? I've tried, in what follows, to set out the main constituents of a home where a household can belong, beginning from the most physical characteristics of the spaces we seek to inhabit.

A Place to Belong and Call Home

In this first section I want to look at four factors that are essential if the place we live in is to have the necessary qualities for it to be capable of being described as a home.

Availability and exclusivity

One of the most basic factors of a home is that we can exclude from it those who do not form part of our household, while ourselves being able to come and go at times of our own choosing. Hot-bedding – as still experienced by some migrant workers with employer-provided accommodation – is not housing. Nor is some temporary bed-and-breakfast accommodation whose management requires the residents to leave the premises for much of the daytime.

Moreover, much of the old dormitory provision has gone from the vast majority of established housing projects, though it still remains in some schemes working with rough-sleepers. However, the increase in street homelessness over recent years has led to many churches being used, perhaps one night a week through the winter months, to accommodate homeless people in halls or worship spaces. The lack of exclusivity and the requirement to move on each morning means that many street-sleepers prefer shop doorways or car parks except during the worst winter weather. On a positive note, the churches providing single-night accommodation (usually on a rota with other churches in the area) seem to take seriously the nature of the welcome they offer. Respectful conversation and the sharing of meals can mitigate some of the alienating factors of the accommodation itself.

Security and protection

I need, when I go out of the place I want to think of as home, to be confident that my possessions, however limited they may be, will be reasonably safe in my absence. I also need some degree of protection against others being able to evict me without strong cause. The ability to lock the doors behind me is crucial, as is some form of tenancy security. Except in the gravest of situations, should it be necessary for my occupancy to be terminated, I need adequate notice. This is both for me to appeal the decision, should I so wish, and also to give me time to find somewhere else to live. Stories are far less common in the UK nowadays of tenants being harassed into leaving their home in order to allow the landlord or owner of the land to sell the property vacant, or to demolish it. However, this practice is still widespread in some developing nations, especially where poor dwellings, whose occupants often have little by way of formal documentation, lie on urban land that has strong commercial development potential. A number of Christian development charities now see advocacy work in such situations, in partnership with local churches, as an important strand of their mission.

Health and safety

During a recent visit to a large African capital city, I was taken to an area where illegally evicted households had created a new shanty, on the edge of a rubbish dump. The smell was beyond description; illness and infestation were endemic. When the rainy season came, water-borne diseases would run rife through the settlement. Ironically, the best chance for the situation being improved lies where it did for the working people of industrial Britain in the early Victorian years. The places where the Africans I visited live and work are sufficiently close to the homes of the wealthier classes that, without remedial action, disease will pass easily to the latter. Without basic safety, a dwelling will never be a home.

Health and safety remain concerns at the lower ends of the UK housing stock. The risk is likely to be greatest where premises have multiple, short-term occupants. An ecumenical project I helped set up in the 1990s was designed to help young, single, benefit claimants in the town access private-sector, rented accommodation. One of the marks of its success was that, in return for promising landlords a good deal, we were able to require a robust health-and-safety inspection of the premises, and the completion of remedial works, before admitting a property to the scheme.

Affordability and sustainability

A house is not a home unless its inhabitants can reliably pay the costs associated with living in it, and do so on a long-term basis. Tenancies break down, again and again, in Britain because of debt. Most housing costs – rent, fuel, water charges, council tax – are not individually huge, but they have to be paid on a frequent basis. It is tempting for tenants to be over-optimistic about the levels of payment they can afford, and then to fall slowly into deeper and deeper arrears across a range of charges. Where personal circumstances change adversely, a previously affordable home can become unsustainable.

Reducing benefits to working-age tenants who have spare bedrooms in social housing, or imposing a total benefit cap on larger households, is predicated on maximising the occupancy of a limited resource and increasing the incentives to find work. Both these aims may be laudable in themselves, but the substantive effect of the policies directed towards them is not. A very high proportion of households affected contain an individual with a disability, while the majority of individuals in such properties are in fact children. Those who move face huge costs of relocation and often find themselves then cast adrift from the informal social and neighbour networks that have helped to sustain them so far. An ever-tightening benefits regime is likely to lead to increased numbers of households forced away from places they know.

There must be a role for Christian and church groups in seeking to identify the displaced and to befriend and help them settle into their new homes.

A Home among Others
In this second section attention is turned to three factors that explore the more human dimension of a home: the people with whom we belong both in our household and as we engage with wider society.

Part of a chosen household
In 1966, the TV film *Cathy Come Home*, directed by Ken Loach, shocked the UK with its depiction of a young family being split up by homelessness, and led directly to the growth of the housing association movement. The right of couples and families to form households of their own choosing, and to be supported to stay together, is a very basic one. For children whose parents do not live together, but who seek to share in their upbringing, it is no longer a right that can be taken for granted.

So, for example, a father or mother who looks after their children for almost half the time will, under the 'bedroom tax' rules, be deducted housing benefit for the rooms those children sleep in, as only one property is allowed to be their home. However, if that parent moves to a smaller property, where the children do not have a bedroom, then it may be considered that they should not be allowed to stay overnight as the accommodation is inadequate. Church-run foodbanks are often the essential component in allowing such families to stretch their income a little further, so that the loss of benefits can be absorbed without driving the family apart.

Members of a diverse community
Outside of the building in which we dwell lies the community that forms our friends and neighbours. The concept of neighbourliness is central to Christian thinking; we need to live in a place where we can both give to and receive from those around us. For most of us, that means that there are a reasonable number of people similar to ourselves living nearby. But a community that has little by way of diversity – be it in terms of age, ethnicity, social class, ability, or whatever – does not provide the full balance within which we can support one another. We belong not just with those very like ourselves but also with those whose needs and abilities complement our own. Those of us who are part of worshipping Christian communities know how much stronger we are for this measure of diversity; what the American author Robert

Putnam has referred to as 'bridging social capital'.

There can often be a negative reaction towards the construction of new housing developments that would widen the social mix of an area, especially if the perception is that poorer people will move into the new properties. Church members themselves are not immune from such initial reactions. However, the church community has a vital part to play in seeing that the social fabric of the community is first sustained, and then stretched wide enough to welcome newcomers.

Accessing and contributing to the wider community

We work, we shop, we play, we study, we worship. Human life is full of interactions with others that take place outside of the home. An essential part of the place we can belong to and call home is that we can access all those dimensions of life from it without that becoming overly expensive or difficult. Some of Britain's most struggling communities are those that were built far away from other population centres, to service a specific industry that no longer provides a major source of employment in the area. Affordable and frequent public transport has an important role to play in sustaining accessibility, as also has the provision of a good range of services – schools, churches, leisure facilities, meeting halls – within the local community itself. The church can again be a major partner in providing space for community activities, as well as providing a large proportion of the volunteers who keep many of them going. Equally, Christians can play their part in keeping local shops viable, sustaining the local school and using the buses.

When I was opening a refugee community centre in the Midlands some years ago, one of my fellow speakers was a member of one of the communities that would have its home within the building. He spoke briefly but movingly of how this was the first day since his arrival in the UK that he felt he was able to be the host rather than the guest, and to offer us hospitality in a place that was his and not ours. And it meant a great deal to him. As Christians we can learn to accept the hospitality of others; to be those who are blessed both as givers and receivers. We only truly belong in a place when our own ability to contribute to the well-being of others is accepted and recognised.

Chapter 2

A History of British Housing Development

Andrew Francis

During the last millennium, a huge shift in housing in British society occurred. In the Anglo-Saxon era, most people lived in either hovels or clan-houses, with sleeping platforms for couples at the edge, while children slept communally close to the central fire. Over centuries, it was only the rich who had 'rooms' where they were separated from their servants, who undertook the menial, domestic work. The vast majority, that is 'the poor', lived in single-room dwellings, be it the Scottish but 'n' ben or the hut or cottage. It was only during the post-Industrial Revolution period that unit mass-housing with cellular rooms became the norm in a tenement or terrace. The reason was simple – it was cheaper for the poor to heat small rooms, therefore they required lower wages! Housing and economics are inter-related.

After 1750, the face of Britain's population and demography substantially changed due to two factors: one was the Highland Clearances in Scotland and the other was the Industrial Revolution. But it also changed the way the populace lived – and the houses they lived in. The purpose of this chapter is to highlight post-1750 historic developments, which require fuller explanation in later chapters, while offering comment or probing some of the issues and questions raised by such developments.

The years 1746–50 saw the end of the Jacobite Uprisings and start of the Highland Clearances. This was the brutal, enforced clearing of the populace from the Highlands by the new chieftains and landowners, culminating in two great waves of exodus around 1790, and more in 1822. People were replaced by sheep, and Scots reliant on subsistence agriculture suffered with several potato famines (just as the Irish also had). Some emigrated to north America and Australasia but a significant majority migrated southwards or eastwards towards the incoming industries or coastal towns. The political 'hurts' of that era are still with us: in 2015, less than one thousand people own and control over 80 per cent of Scotland – a different kind of feudalism, creating the widespread call for 'land reform'.[1]

The Industrial Revolution changed the face of England, southern Wales and lowland Scotland. Instead of a predominantly agricultural economy, urbanisation around regional industries, each with their own style of factories, replaced small market towns and cathedral cities. Josiah Wedgwood, the philanthropic Potteries 'magnate', recalled his childhood memory of how previously: 'The labourers eked out a bare subsistence from wretched plots of land and lived in huts.'[2] Thomson's research noted: 'Despite all that can be said as to the unplanned jerry-building and profiteering that went on in the growing industrial towns, the houses themselves were better than those to which many immigrants from the countryside had been accustomed.'[3] Even better were the mill developments of Robert Owen at New Lanark, Scotland or of Titus Salt at Saltaire in Yorkshire, where not only housing but welfare schemes and schools were provided for workers and their children.

Previously, although merchants and some artisans lived in market towns, Britain's economy and housing was predominantly agrarian. Only landowners or verderers in the royal forests had any notional housing 'rights'. Following the 1707 Acts of Union, the lifestyle and fortification of the Border Reivers (clan families holding territory on the Scottish borders[4]) demonstrated clearly that housing was something held only by force or status, and could be easily lost.

Two Responses: Tenements and Terraces

In the growing urbanisation of Scotland and England, two different Victorian styles of development were created to accommodate the increasing density of necessary populations, within walking access of their workplaces of industrial production. In Scotland, this style was the tenement, whereas in England it was the terraced house, which also ribboned out into industrial South Wales through Cardiff, Swansea and Llanelli, traversing northward up the valleys.

Tenements

Anyone who has travelled in northern Europe, the Baltic ports or Scandinavia will be just as familiar with tenements as urban Scots are. All Scotland's major cities – Aberdeen, Dundee, Edinburgh, Glasgow, Inverness, Perth, Stirling – became tenemental. At the 2011 Census, over 22 per cent of Scots still lived in tenements, as against 0.002 per cent of English, most of whom were in Newcastle-upon-Tyne. Scots tenement blocks often had shops and offices on the ground floor with six to ten flats evenly spread on the upper floors around a central stair-well. The tenement is still as vibrant a model of UK housing as any other – lest southerners forget.

'North of the border families in cities have tended to live in flats not houses, sharing space in a predesigned (not converted) way . . . Scots have tended to rent not own for most of the last century.'[5] 'Scots tended to live in council-owned, not private property . . . Scottish housing conditions within living memory were more squalid, life-shortening and overcrowded than anywhere else in these islands . . . Housing has carved the face of Scotland, the limits of hope and the pace of social endeavour.'[6] By 1911, Glasgow had a greater housing/population density than London and until 1951 Glasgow's percentage population growth grew twice as fast as London's. In 1951, Glasgow still suffered a known 50 per cent overcrowding rate compared with the 5 per cent overcrowding rate in London.

But most Scottish tenements began life with shared outside sanitation in communal garden spaces behind the tenement block. In 1965, 40 per cent of Glasgow's housing stock had no hot-water supply nor plumbed-in bath/shower and 20 per cent had no inside toilet.[7] The fight for their modernisation and resident control is eloquently and humanly told by a Scots architect, Raymond Young, who not only campaigned but also moved his wife and family into a Glasgow tenement.[8] He went on to become Director Scotland for the Housing Corporation, and is the contributor of Chapter 7 about the lessons and stresses surrounding rural housing and infrastructure provision. We should note that UK funding has not followed the exciting lead of our European partners, in further refurbishing tenements with shared heating systems, eco-gardens, rooftop solar panels and bicycle parks as well as play-space. Tenements basically are a green alternative, and *can* inexpensively be improved to become even greener.

Terraces

Much English Victorian housing development was unregulated. Whether it was for the mills of the Pennine counties, for shipbuilding and the associated heavy industry of Merseyside or the north-east, workers were needed in great numbers. Some industrialists paid as cheaply as they could for rows of terraced houses (think *Coronation Street*), packing in as many workers and their families as possible. The overloading on each street's basic sanitation brought death and disease, as did the smog and the smoke. In some towns, the municipality had to step in as the influx of rural workers and the lack of available housing meant folks squatted, camped and hutted in even less sanitary conditions upon any open space. It was the pioneering 1866 Liverpool Act, which that municipality promulgated in order to regulate housing density, that statutorily demanded a minimum level of 'privy provision'.

By 1831, there was a civic master-plan to develop the city of Leeds, which was predicated on one infamous form of terraced house – the back-to-back. So, 'in the next eighty years, some 17000 houses surrounded the factories, railway yards, gasworks and brickyards, and the absence of villas and middle class housing gave a fearful monotony to acres of brick-built back-to-backs'.[9] Often between six and ten people lived in each back-to-back. Leeds Council knew quickly that they had allowed unregulated development, and so promoted their own 1870 Improvement Act (modelled on Liverpool's of 1866) to rectify this. Several other now-major cities had to use a similar legislative process to improve their own housing stocks, sanitation, and so on, too.

Leeds' problems remained as demolition caused overcrowding elsewhere and in 1900 that city desperately resorted 'to the Scottish solution', building two tenement blocks to temporarily rehouse tenants while high-density back-to-backs were demolished. This required the power of the English national (there were exemptions for Scotland and Wales) 1890 Housing of the Working Classes Act, to effect the necessary compulsory purchase of land. It says everything that 1909's national Housing and Town Planning Act banned the further building of back-to-backs. Yet over a century later, back-to-backs are still bought and sold and (once modernised) *do* remain comfortable homes across Yorkshire.

Birmingham, Manchester/Salford, Merseyside, Sheffield and the north-east had learned quickly and, while reliant on much terraced housing, always built them with backyards and often their own 'outside lavvy'. Although some back-to-backs can be found in Sunderland and a few other northern, once industrialised towns, they were a much lower proportion of the total than in Leeds and West Yorkshire. Such high-density development created the need for city parks, including play-space as 'lungs' for the people; we return to this 'open space usage' in Chapter 6 by Helen Woolley, who is a practical advocate and trusted expert in this subject.

The very presence of such open spaces, as well as later allotments (finally secured by Atlee's 1950 Allotment Act), provided a good quality of life in a crowded city, which has meant that many cities still rely on their well-built Victorian terraces, and their later Edwardian versions, to provide homes for couples (old or young), first-time buyers and newly-arriving immigrants. It was only the call of God, through the demands of a seminary, that dragged me away from my first house purchase of a Sparkbrook, Birmingham, terraced home, with its nearby park, library and allotment.

The Garden City Movement's Agenda

The garden-city concept was first envisaged in 1898 by Ebenezer Howard, in the book now known as *Garden Cities of Tomorrow*.[10] Howard planned that garden cities would have appropriately proportioned amounts of housing, industry and 'greenspace' (for agriculture, allotments and parks) arranged in a concentric pattern covering about 6,000 acres for 32,000 residents. Howard quickly founded the Garden City Association (later known as the Town and Country Planning Association) and, using funds from his book's success, helped set up Letchworth Garden City. 1919 saw the second in Welwyn Garden City but the movement stalled, as blue-collar workers could afford neither to buy nor to rent the houses. Others, noting Howard's ideas, set up garden suburbs such as Hampstead (London), which increasingly attracted wealthy homeowners, or Wavertree (Liverpool), which attracted private investors who bought the smaller semis for rental purposes.

The out-pricing of workers via either high purchase prices or large rental costs defied Howard's original vision for both Welwyn and Letchworth. He saw each of these 32,000 strong 'cities' (his word) as satellites of larger, probably pre-existing cities, all connected by low-cost, rapid rail-transit, to allowing the 'working man and his family' both mobility and a good quality of life.

> And because the people in their collective capacity own the land on which this beautiful group of cities is built, the public buildings, the churches, the schools and universities, the libraries, picture galleries, theatres would be on a scale of magnificence, which no city in the world whose land is in pawn to private investors can afford.[11]

It took the Christian Quaker families of the Cadburys, in Birmingham's Bournville, and the Rowntrees in York to break the mould and actually create economical, local, garden suburbs, with quality housing for their workers. Acknowledging the biblical injunction that every family should 'sit under their own vine and fig-tree' (Mic. 4:4; Zech. 3:10), they planted all the gardens of those houses with the English equivalent: apple and pear trees. Helen Woolley writes about the influence of Bournville life in Chapter 6.

Collectivism and affordability were at the heart of Howard's vision of what makes a garden city, but in his November 2015 Spending Review, Chancellor Osborne made no reference to promoting Howard-style collective ownership in his stated desire to expand the the Ebbsfleet Garden City in Kent.

Post-First World War

The twenty years between European-rooted global conflicts saw huge and often unresolved conflicts in British society. Although the 1894 Finance Act had unified the effect, purpose and execution of five different forms of estate duty, the punitive effects of Asquith's 1914 'estate duty' were delayed by the advent of the First World War. But afterwards, the break-up of large, titled family estates gathered apace as parcels of land or tied housing was sold off to meet this taxation while the UK economy enjoyed a brief boom.

Such economic well-being saw the 1919 Housing Act, which enabled municipal authorities to undertake a new surge in house-building, with increased powers of development, planning and compulsory purchase. Learning from Victorian mistakes, this brought into being slightly larger terraced homes. Such typical Edwardian terraces had nominal front gardens, and hallways, as well as larger rooms and backyards.

As the great rural estates shrank in number and size, 'live-in' domestic service and former patterns of estate/farm-workers' paternalistic retention of tied dwellings diminished, and class divisions deepened as the general populace read of different regions' needs, hearing about the excesses of the rich aristocracy or the Bloomsbury Set. They also learned of national growing poverty, leading to the hunger marches of the 1920s, most famously culminating in the 1936 Jarrow March. Insanitary and overcrowded urban housing, with no local opportunities to grow food, were at the heart of urban impoverishment.

In Chapter 3, Sean Gardiner details how municipal local authorities shouldered a huge burden in assuming responsibility for much of their town or city's social housing. Private landlords increasingly retreated to buy the better-quality middle-class suburban homes being built between the wars; Wavertree in Liverpool and Stainbeck in Leeds both provide strong examples of such rental areas. The Allotments Act of 1922 properly amended the initial 1908 legislation, allowing any householder (not just the owner) to apply for a small regulated parcel of designated land to grow their own vegetables or flowers. These were significant changes in the nature and face of the towns and suburbs of Britain. Each in their own way helped prepare the nation for World War II, with its aerial bombardments, loss of skilled contractors and 'Dig for Victory' campaign.

Britain's social conscience was alive and well between the wars. The philanthropic development of garden suburbs – whether in Hampstead, London, or Bournville, Birmingham, Port Sunlight on Merseyside, Dennistoun, Glasgow, or Westerton, Dunbartonshire – told of a desire to create good-quality housing areas to positively affect the nature and life of the residents. The famous 1930s 'Peckham Experiment' demonstrated the effect of environment upon health.[12] Nearly a thousand local families paid one shilling (5p!) per week to join the Pioneer Health Centre, with its social spaces, 'gymnasia' and workshops, ultimately moving into architect-designed purpose-built premises. Regrettably, lessons learned from this project did not remain in the minds of post-war civic planners.

Post-War Developments[13]

World War II had seen the Ministry of War gradually requisition land and resources. Post-war development and (later) Cold War fears led to it accruing more. In 2015, the Land Registry confirmed that the now-renamed Ministry of Defence holds about 1 per cent of all UK land.

The immediate aftermath of war involved food- and furniture-rationing for several years. In 1947, much-heralded modern, but questionably coherent, town-and-country planning legislation addressed the previous lack of complementary planning laws. Further major social change included the inception of the NHS in 1948, and an increasing national pride, which was exemplified by the 1951 Festival of Britain.

Different needs – different responses

All these developments produced regional civic demand to expand urbanisation with further growth of edge-of-town local authority estates of rental housing, such as those of Eyres Monsell in Leicester, or Kirby New Town (as in *Z-Cars*), near Liverpool, or Halton Moor, Leeds, in the 1950s, and Wythenshawe outside Manchester, or Birmingham's Chelmsley Wood, in the 1960s.[14] It also led to huge inner-city urban regeneration in both massive housing projects and tower blocks, still extant today.

The role of the 'pre-fab' should not be forgotten. These single-storeyed, small, two-bedroomed, poorly insulated, asbestos-roofed dwellings were deemed to have a ten-year life. Some are still in use today but most have been modernised with the addition of new roofs, good insulation, brick cladding, and central heating to replace the old coal-fired back boiler. Today, Catford's (London) 'Excalibur' estate and parts of Bristol have fine examples of ongoing modernised prefab usage – a tribute to their original design quality.

'In 1945, housing need was massive. In Glasgow, a quarter of a million people were on the council house waiting list.'[15] The 1945 Bruce Report recommended that Glasgow's inner city be rebuilt. Glasgow's civic leaders won their battle against Westminster politicians who wanted that *whole* populace to move out to create new towns, such as Cumbernauld and East Kilbride. A programme of clearance, demolition and rebuilding began, including the (in)famous Gorbals tenement blocks, inevitably involving having to rehouse some families in large, impersonal estates, such as Drumchapel and Easterhouse, on opposite sides of the city. But true to the spirit of Raymond Young and many other community activists, the real improvement in these newer estates and refurbished tenements occurred when local residents were empowered to form housing co-operatives, enabling Glasgow by 1991 to be the UK leader in various forms of such resident-led housing control. But that jumps ahead of our history . . .

As a heavily bombed capital city, London had to make post-war decisions about rebuilding housing for its residents and workers, just as some industries chose to relocate away from London. The revitalisation of rail lines to either newer or expanding older towns led to the 1950s and onwards development of inexpensive housing for commuting skilled workers in places like Stevenage or Hitchin or Tonbridge. Some towns deliberately sought to accommodate 'the London overspill'. One 1950s example is the northern-edge-of-Swindon greenfield development of the Penhill estate, with its broad tree-lined streets, low-rent houses with gardens, community paddling pool, and park with tennis courts, housing self-exiling, skilled, blue-collar Londoners.[16]

One needs to recall that until the 1888, when various acts of Parliament cohered to create the London County Council, with power over 117 square miles, London had existed as self-governing boroughs (evidenced even today by the village 'feel' of many neighbourhood high streets). That 'wartime spirit', the bombing, 'Dig for Victory' and the royal family's visits pulled many London boroughs towards their bigger identity. As 19 per cent of London's East End had been razed to the ground by the German Luftwaffe and much infrastructure had been bomb-damaged, a new plan was needed. Professor Patrick Abercrombie (hence 'the Abercrombie Plan') used Birmingham as a practical model, suggesting that London redefine itself as four concentric rings of housing, settlement, differing population densities and economic life.[17] This was enforced by the Town and Country Act of 1947 resulting in 'an experiment in urban living . . . the popularity of the tower block. Some 400 were erected in London during the 1960s.'[18] The impact of that upon London's cityscape and future are discussed in Chapter 5, written by Helen Roe, a London-based architect.

Of course, there were often industry-associated housing developments. The railway works in Crewe, York and Swindon determined the patterns of worker-housing growth. David Smith, the economist, wrote of his Darlaston childhood: 'Many worked for Rubery Owen . . . it employed 17000 people . . . providing sports facilities, day nurseries . . . and Rubery Owen rented houses to its workers.'[19] Without the same paternalism, the numbers of car-industry workers forced the further development of Longbridge, Rubery and West Heath, in Birmingham, as well as that of Hailwood, near Liverpool, and the outer ring of Coventry.

In the thirty years from 1948, the UK built at least 100,000 council houses per annum, occasionally pushing 250,000 units, but this virtually stopped after 1978, which immediately halted the growth of housing stock. It is not coincidental that Thatcher and the Tories were elected in 1979. These figures should not be lost when recalling that, in spring 2015, Chancellor Osborne declared that to build 150,000 new homes 'by 2020' would be a hard task. Post-war housing policy was now subject to party-political resolve, not need.

Some of those 1960s inner-city housing projects gained notoriety. Built inexpensively (critics would say cheaply), they crammed together housing units, with poor insulation for both sound and heat, little social space and few other community provisions. Sometimes unwittingly, rather than as policy decisions, they often become 'sink estates' for the poorest of the poor, socially needy or otherwise marginalised such as single parents or people who were mentally ill. The huge estates of Hulme in Manchester or Byker in Newcastle-upon-Tyne or North Peckham in London have all had media-documented difficulties or criminal activity associated with overcrowding – as have similar urban communities elsewhere (although proving direct causality is a legal matter). In each of these examples, events have brought positive social change.

- Hulme became infamous for its poorly built, multi-storey, deck-access flats, called 'The Crescents' with their expensive-to-run underfloor heating and crime-ridden, long, common landings which ultimately had to be destroyed in sections in order to refurbish the flats at 'higher spec' for onward sale or rent to high-salaried city workers. 'The Crescents' have now been demolished to make way for low-rise housing.

- Byker, with a population in five figures but the smallest percentage of car ownership in Newcastle, was epitomised by its petty crime and car theft as well as the iconic Byker Wall flats. Recently the whole estate has received cash injections for property refurbishment, and crime figures are dropping.

- With one of the highest European rates of social casualty, Peckham attracted European Union funding from 1990 for its planned and widespread rebuilding, which increased in speed and subsidy following the murder of 10-year-old Nigerian immigrant, Damilola Taylor, in 2000.

Is it too simplistic to say that if folk are enabled to have decent houses in which to make homes and develop pride in their neighbourhood, then social cohesion and a sense of community are improved?

The New Alternatives: Squatting, Hutting and Mouseholing

Big cities from the late 1950s suffered varying measures of unoccupied residential property, which obviously belonged to private owners waiting to sell, local authorities and either institutional or private landlords. In the face of rising homelessness, the challenge of TV drama *Cathy Come Home*, youth migration or middle-class idealists inspired by Banks' *L-Shaped Room* and Delaney's kitchen-sink drama, *A Taste of Honey*, theatre and TV as well as fiction were pointing up the scale of 1960s housing problems. The paucity of quality rental properties, the fickleness of private landlords and empty, potentially decaying properties, demanded action . . . and led many into squatting.

Squatting
Squatting involved potentially illegal entry into a property, then its

occupation. Responsible squatters would immediately offer a fair rent to the landlord or owner and become responsible for the payment of utility bills. Squatting in large properties often involved multiple occupation with each resident or couple having their own bedsit, while sharing communal facilities. Often squatters would repaint and repair premises, tidying up back gardens to provide children's play-space or communal eating. Not all squatting *need* be deemed as morally wrong.

Sometimes communes, extended families and mutual-interest groups shared a squat because there was no other housing of sufficient size available. For others, it was experiencing squatting that gathered a group to buy and share communal housing; one example is the now rural-based commune, known as the Shrubb Family, in Norfolk.[20] Sometimes, it was the size of the squat which generated mutual interest that evolved through a gradual change of residents. An example of this is that in the 1960s, squatters occupied many of the large houses in Notting Hill, London, or Moseley, Birmingham, which are now desirable addresses. Several gradually lost their squatters, were then quickly refurbished and brought back to either the rental or sale market; effectively, squatting had brought those houses back into use.

This was even more true of smaller family homes, as this explanation from the experience of one of the 1970s Birmingham Squatters Action Team demonstrates:

Speed was essential. Some owners deliberately sent contractors to put cement or concrete down the WC, then smash the upper pan, kitchen and bathroom sinks with a sledgehammer and break the fusebox and stop-cock, to stop the squatters, rendering the house uninhabitable for months. So normally, two people would effect entry to a house, a folding stool enabled ease over the back yard wall and a domestic knife blade would slide the lock from a downstairs sash window. One person remained silently in the house, while the other went and alerted the van and supporters around the corner [no mobile phones then!]. The silent occupant would let the supporters in and then leave; if the police arrived, no one at the property was legally guilty of 'breaking and entering'. The supporters would quickly put up curtains, plug in a fridge, wire in a cooker, set out a lounge with battery powered lamps, fireside chairs and rugs, while others put up beds. Within an hour already pajama-ed children and older folk would be brought by car to get in those made up beds to continue their night's sleep. When the police arrived, they were reminded that 'everyone had come in through an opened door', informed this was an official squat (only a civil offence) and told of the sleeping children's presence, forcing the police to involve somnolent Social Services if they wished to take more action than drink the mugs of tea proffered. Overnight the locks would be changed, preventing the owner's access but the very next morning, they would receive a letter offering a fair rent, while utility companies were also contacted to make deposit payments.

Quite often absentee landlords would then agree to sell the property to a sympathetic housing association, enabling the tenancy to continue and another homeless family remain rehoused. This pattern of action and response severally occurred in London, Birmingham, Manchester, Leeds, Sheffield and Newcastle. Scottish cities were far more immune to urban squatting because of the prevalence of tenements. Urban squatters became particularly creative in challenging officialdom.

Perhaps the most famous early squat was in London, becoming known as 'Frestonia' after one of its main constituent roads. It developed as an artists' and residents' colony, applying for separate UN recognition as a country while all those involved legally changed their surnames to Bramley – after another of the constituent roads – meaning that, should the local authority evict them, they would have to be rehoused together as one family! Ultimately the council had to facilitate them to become the Bramley Housing Association, which to this day is still managed by the Notting Hill Housing Trust.

Another of the largest London 'squats' was in Peckham in the former DHSS, previously Camberwell Labour Exchange, building. It was occupied 24/7 by a group of (predominantly underground) musicians and community activists, who bedded down after the upstairs gig-room and rehearsal spaces had quietened. While using one of their meeting spaces, I discovered (then regularly supported) their on-site vegan café until they were all evicted in late 1990. Something similar developed in the 'squat' in Soho's 12Bar in Denmark Street, London, which ended in a much more violent 2015 eviction. Such high-profile cases highlight the issues.

One is tempted to observe that, if either central government departments or big institutional landlords leave commercial premises unoccupied for lengthy periods of time, 'community-minded' squatters provide a necessary challenge about a multi-use cityscape. A broader observation is that as squatting increasingly returns to London, often through a new set of 'Generation Rent' idealists, it is indicative of high rents and fewer affordable homes. In 2012, squatting became illegal in residential properties, thus challenging multi-use patterns for other city property. But, in reality, squatting is a sign of homelessness for many; the majority of squatters, often with less legal nous than idealists, are desperately poor, or unemployed and needy. 'The decision to squat is not a moral one for most people, let alone political; it's a necessity.'[21]

Britain lags far behind its European counterparts in creating 'quality of life' accommodation. Many city-apartment dwellers in Stockholm, Sweden and other Scandinavian cities have some form of accessible rural retreat suitable for weekend and summer usage. The Russian example of the *dacha* or the German *Gartenschreber* are well known. My former French neighbours used to return each weekend from their sophisticated city flats to (sometimes primitive) village family homes, just to enjoy space, fresher air, vegetable patches and rural life. When I lived in Liverpool, I shared the rent and overnight midweek usage of an old showman's wagon with four weekending inner-city families. The wagon was kept in a blackberry-hedged Wirral field with other such shared wagons. The creative use of such rural retreats can compensate for smaller living spaces in geographically pressured cities.

Hutting

Generally, we need look no further than Scotland for both an admirable example and a prophetic lead in the movement called 'hutting'. Celebrated in art, music and poetry, rustic simple buildings are part of Scotland's landscape and culture, ranging from shepherds' bothies, island crofts and Highland shielings. Hutting in Scotland began as a working-class response to the need for rural space close to the cramped and industrialised cities. Like Russian *dacha*s, these basic, hand-built huts, set upon a rural vegetable patch or fringe-of-town allotment, have become a vital part of many Scottish families' lives. Only Scotland-oriented readers will understand the significance of *The Broons*' but 'n' ben to their family life. However, for generations, hutting was risky because nearby landowners wanted access and/ or residence restricted as they perceived 'hutting' as a form of illicit squatting.

Thanks to the pioneering work of the ReForesting Scotland organisation, and their varied supporters, policies are changing. Subject to a 30-square-metre size restriction and 'treading lightly upon the land', many of the governmental or legal barriers to hutting are being lifted since June 2014. ReForesting Scotland is currently in the midst of a campaign to enable one thousand new hutters, either couples or families, to take to the land. Encouragingly, they are working to help both unemployed and working-class hutters just as much, if not more, to return hutting to its 'roots among the people'. Equally pleasing is the supportive Scottish media coverage of the 'hutting movement' and positive analysis by social commentators.

The social diversity of hutters is notable, ranging from those urbanites who effectively create small overnight shelters on allotments to those individuals and couples relishing the call of the wild in rural isolation. There are also hutters gathering small settlements, essentially creating small, temporary communities as well as those using eco- or alternative building methods to the usual 'glorified shed'-type construction. What is clear is that hutting, set alongside urban higher-density living, is but one strategy to create a better quality of life for participants as well as to enable smaller urban living spaces.

Two English expressions of hutting have been that of the rural commune and of (not necessarily but often New Age) travellers. An example of the former is that of the Tinker's Bubble community in Somerset, where dwellers live 'fossil-fuel free', off-grid in their own hand-built shelters, monthly paying both a monetary rent and three days of community-work on the land around them. The shameful and violent attacks by Wiltshire police upon the Peace Convoy travelling community in 1985 resulted in the Battle of the Beanfield;[22] in turn this exposed the Establishment's rejection of those seeking alternative housing or lifestyles and has driven many into solo journeying or some alternative settlement. The number of people living on narrowboats, in Gypsy vardas or settled in yurts or small-eco-communities – such as the various Welsh versions of Tipi Valley and Brithdir Mawr – continues to grow. Media estimates believe over 125,000 people have such alternative lifestyles.

Mouseholing

The desire for a quality of living is underlined by the growing trend called 'mouseholing'. This pattern was noted, first just after the Millennium, among 'empty-nester' couples, who would sell up their large family home to buy both a smaller property in their work location and a small bolt-hole elsewhere. Many of them had originally had more bedrooms in their initial, larger property than in the subsequent two smaller properties together. This was quite different from traditional second- or holiday-home ownership.

Talking about this at a recent conference in Yorkshire, two couples described their own mouseholing. The first couple now have a central Leeds flat and a tiny, one-bedroomed, terraced bolt-hole in Whitby; while the second London-based couple moved into their daughter's 'granny-flat annexe', spending their holidays and 'three-day weekends' at a cottage in the dales.

As housing stock increases, this could be another strategy to be encouraged in liberating family accommodation that now exceeds its owners' needs. In 2015, if broadsheet newspapers and BBC Radio 4 are to be believed, well over 300,000 couples or individuals are mouseholing, meaning between 4 and 5 per cent of the UK population are part of this growing trend. However, in marked contrast to hutters, mouseholers fall into the same category as second-home owners as they take two housing units from the market; hutters live in one housing unit but create or build an informal accommodation space for the years of their family's hutting.

In 2015, the local council declared that 51 per cent of Coniston's housing are second homes – with all the consequent issues for the local economy and education. Other Lake District, East Anglian and West Country communities face similar levels of second homes. As people of faith become active in the housing lobby, they need to (at least) review why they believe that anyone has the right to occupy two housing units when so many others struggle to achieve 'housing security' – whether owned or rented.

Squatting, hutting or mouseholing all require creativity and taking a non-mainstream view of housing needs. Each questions society's general view that 'bigger is better', enabling both 'churn' within the housing stock and better urban density of population. Alongside these, those who take a more 'alternative' or communal view of housing provision together are providing significant ideas about the nature of future housing and planning controls.

Rachmann and Poulson

One of the contributory factors which encouraged many squatters of my acquaintance was the rapacious greed of some private landlords or the seeming corruption of a few influential elected councillors in the provision of local authority housing. Two names stand out.

Peter Rachman (1919–62) was a flamboyant businessman, who ran a west London property empire. He owned many of the Notting Hill properties that were later occupied by squatters. He became notorious for driving out long-established tenants, by dubious (some would say appalling and illegal) means, and installing newer residents at much higher rents because the latter were not subject to rent controls. Rachman's exploits became public only after the investigation of the Profumo affair in 1963 exposed his business tactics, but they were sufficiently bad that the *Concise Oxford English Dictionary* continues to list 'Rachmanism' as 'the exploitation and intimidation of tenants by unscrupulous landlords'.

John Poulson (1910–92) was an architectural designer, who used his business acumen, hard work and good family connections to create global contracts. He specialised in creating projects on paper, combining both architecture and design, before selling that 'package' on to major builders, local authorities and government departments who shouldered the financial and trading risks of developing them: a brilliantly successful model. Poulson's business relationship with T. Dan Smith, the ambitious leader of Newcastle-upon-Tyne Council, led to it all unravelling. A history of apparent bribes, court cases with guilty verdicts, prison sentences and disgraced politicians, including T. Dan Smith and then Home Secretary Reginald Maudling, demonstrated to many the corruption within the contracts for the building and supervision of much local authority rental-housing provision. What happened in the north-east gained notoriety but had national significance as people increasingly looked to home ownership rather than to renting.

Bland Suburbia and Individualism

Between the world wars, a pattern of outer-ring, predominantly semi-detached housing was built for the burgeoning middle classes. The suburbs were arriving, at the inexpensive ends of London's Tube lines and in dependent towns such as Stockport's Heatons developments or Birmingham's infill estates, including Weoley Castle. They were often built in a standard style, with both front and back gardens.

By the late 1960s, several national house-builders had their own recognisable styles and often worked in tandem rapidly and inexpensively to develop large swathes of new housing for the private owner, often infilling suburban farmland. One example is in Swindon, where houses were built upon the former water meadows between Swindon's northern boundary and that Penhill estate. The newly developed area,

Greenmeadow, attracted many Penhill residents with the cheap mort-gages of that era. But the Greenmeadow builders had worked in the same combination some ten years before in Wigton Moor, Leeds, and did so again ten years later in St Neot's and Cambourne, East Anglia, making all three places look the same, creating a bland identity. This pattern was replicated across many English suburbs, with their simi-lar-looking primary schools and parades of local shops.

By the 2000s, encouraged by all manner of TV property pro-grammes, owners were 'improving' their properties to put their indi-vidual stamp upon them. The addition of loft rooms, extensions, clad-ding and conservatories may have caused planners headaches, but not the distress caused by suburban flooding, which was assisted by the almost unrestricted hard-landscaping of gardens and driveways. Even older estates, such as Sevenoaks' model Montreal Park area, built ei-ther side of World War II, were not immune to owner-improvements but did have stricter planning control. This was because its original developers built on an A–B–C–D–E pattern with five different house style-and-footprint designs to avoid any sense of bland uniformity as no property owner 'should be able to see another property like theirs'. There are good planning lessons to be learned from Montreal Park's design variations just as much as from Greenmeadow's flooding and its expensive remediation.

One reaction to the strict planning controls of suburbia was multi-ply expressed by HRH Charles, Prince of Wales.[23] His trenchant critique of modernist architecture (such as the National Gallery's 'monstrous carbuncle') is well known but he is also highly critical of suburbia's tight zoning, restricting any other development than small retail units, schools and community halls or churches. His Duchy of Cornwall put these critical principles into practice when, in the 1990s, they devel-oped the six-thousand-strong village of Poundbury, near Dorchester. There, the Duchy adopted a 'no zoning' policy, drawn almost directly from Ebenezer Howard's 'garden city' philosophy, allowing housing, retail, schooling and community facilities to co-exist with light in-dustry or commercial offices. A similarly no-zoned town was built at Fairford Leys, near Aylesbury. But this trend has not continued.

Faith in the City

Faith in the City is the ambiguous name of the report of the Archbishop's Commission on Urban Priority Areas, published in 1985.[24] It caused a political storm and media headlines for days in its declared 'Call to

Church and Nation'. It explained that England's urban malaise and structure of inequality was due to three factors:

- Economic decline;

- Physical decay; and

- Social disintegration;

effectively making two nations – 'the haves and the have-nots'. Its chapter about housing demonstrated how these three factors demanded huge changes in the nature of provision. It emphasised a fourfold agenda for the church – ecumenically – and beyond.

First, there was a need for churches, as the UK's largest source and mobiliser of volunteers, to familiarise themselves with the issues and for church members personally to commit themselves to action. David Walker, now the Bishop of Manchester, who wrote Chapter 1 of this book, has become a nationally accepted commentator on housing issues.

Second, the plight of the homeless, the destitute and those 'falling through the housing net' need support and ministry. One only need think of the work of St Catherine's in Edinburgh, St George's Crypt, in Leeds, Nottingham's central United Reformed churches and St Martin-in-the-Fields in London as a few of the responses of the UK churches to recognise both the ongoing work and its impetus from *Faith in the City*. Place these and other 'homelessness' initiatives alongside the work of the Salvation Army and recognise how much the churches are doing – yet there is more to do.

Third, the report recognised that surplus church land and redundant premises could make way for small-scale housing projects, which would both provide homes and also act as ecumenical encouragers for more such work. Littlemore Baptist Church, Oxford (where eight flats for homeless people were built on land owned by the church), Worthing (Sussex) Churches Homeless Project and south Lancashire's Green Pastures Project all spring to my mind, as does the multi-locational, ecumenical, Housing Justice-inspired Julius Project, providing support to those rehomed by local authorities.

Finally, Christians need to rework a 'theology of housing', which draws on biblical roots, Jesus' teaching and servant-discipleship, to underpin both the call and the need to create a more just society and world. This will in turn require that people are housed appropriately and well, not simply adequately, in patterns that do not break social cohesion nor damage the planet. It will occur through the posing of questions and offering principles for discussion; see Chapter 9, 'Homecoming'.

Housing Action Trusts, Co-Operatives and 'People Together'

In 1988, the Conservative government created six Housing Action Trusts to redevelop the poorest social housing in different UK regions. Apart from North Hull's HAT, which was wound up within a decade, all made huge changes to their area's housing, landscape and provision. Liverpool's HAT demolished over fifty tower blocks, replacing them with low-rise units, and refurbished thirteen more tower blocks, while Castle Vale's HAT (Birmingham) similarly demolished over thirty tower blocks within a few square miles. HATs were finally abolished between 2005 and 2007, with their housing stock being passed to a variety of social landlords, but not always housing associations. The government's decision not to create other HATs in Scotland or Wales either publicly denied that these regions had poor quality housing stock or was a callous political expedience.

There were those who saw HATs as a Tory government measure to squeeze out such local urban initiatives as housing co-operatives. These were often used by individuals seeking to refurbish large for shared usage, with each participant family having their own private space while sharing communal facilities. Examples include Pembrokeshire's Glandwr Community, Gloucestershire's Postlip Hall or Herefordshire's Canon Frome co-households.[25] Many of us who were involved in such co-operatives (even if only as financial supporters) used early housing association legal frameworks to protect both tenants and investors. Using similar ideology and legal frameworks, several groups of self-builders used the housing association model; one famous and much televised self-build group is the Hedgehog Housing Co-operative, near Brighton. Of course, housing associations are also known as mass 'social housing' landlords. So it is appropriate that Chapter 4, by Chris Horton, a leading thinker about housing associations, documents these transitions.

The 'Right to Buy' and the London Factor

It was only the middle classes who had traditionally sought mortgages to buy their own homes. My grandparents' interwar generation only ever thought of renting their homes. Thrift may have enabled a few to buy a small 'final years' home. But following the 'you never had it so good' era of the early 1960s came a symbiosis of private housing and cheap(er than renting) mortgages. This led to the huge suburban developments referred to above.

The first Thatcher government of 1979 instituted the 'right to buy', from 1980, for secure tenants of both local councils and the majority of housing associations, at discounted prices. This was disastrous as, in the next twenty years, 1.5 million properties were sold off from the public housing stock, but hardly any replacements were built from the proceeds. With the effects of an inflationary economy, rising house prices and the easy right of resale many tenants, particularly in London, many buyers made a financial killing. The losers were the poor and those needing the now-gone social housing stock.[26]

In London and other big cities, this generated an even more obvious poverty gap: 'Poverty never leaves London. It just changes its form and appearance.'[27] But new homeowners with money in their pockets became cash-buyers, creating 'gazumping' and a continual rise in city house prices, which continues to have far-reaching consequences.

- Towns on direct, fast rail routes to London found their property prices rising beyond local wage rates as commuters moved in. In Doncaster in Yorkshire, or Northampton, on such rail routes, property prices are 60 per cent to 90 per cent higher than those for comparable properties, twenty-plus miles away, which remain less attractive to London commuters.

- The editor knows an Oxford householder who, having saved up the money to pay the fees involved in moving house, managed to up-scale to Birmingham, where she was able to buy a bigger house, refurbish it and landscape its garden – all thanks to the effect of the 'London factor' on Oxford prices.

- Why is it that many of London's high rise buildings, including the Shard, particularly their higher residential floors, remain 'dark' (i.e. unoccupied) as buyers simply use such unoccupation as a way of creating capital?

The London property boom, originally enhanced by the 'right to buy', is becoming responsible for hyper-inflating property prices and personal wealth for some across southern (and all big city) Britain.

At first, this acts as upward pressure, progressively pushing higher prices further up the housing chain. Then it reverses, so that foreign wealthy investors are among the few who can afford the most expensive houses, which then spiral gradually upwards, thus becoming the engine pulling all the underlying 'tiers' of house price upwards, too. As executive vice-chair of the Mennonite Trust in the UK, I witnessed this all too starkly in 2012 when the trust was seeking a five-bedroomed staff house. The price of a suitable property rose by £35,000 between the morning of our enquiry and that same afternoon's viewing. On that same day I was advising a Radix Community household about buying a four-bedroomed house for £29,000 in Burnley, Lancashire. The disparity of house prices within the UK is now even more enormous.

Part of that disparity is caused by London's seeming immunity to the 2008 global recession, as far as house prices are concerned. Virtually everywhere else beyond London's commuter belts, many newer homeowners found themselves to be in negative equity, as their house prices stalled or dropped. The 'London factor' has further divided Britain. How we begin to deal with the needs and the wants of the whole UK are addressed by Paul Lusk in Chapter 9, as well as in the co-editors' shared vision in Chapter 10.

In July 2015, the UK's National Crime Agency released information[28] showing that 'top-end, highly priced' properties in London and other metropolitan centres are being increasingly used for money laundering. This is done simply by buying a potentially high-value but physically poor property, then paying for its refurbishment by 'importing' many five-figure cash-deposited sums together into a city account. The renovated property is sold at a large profit, creating legitimate sterling funds, which are then dispersed through a variety of shadow accounts. The fact that 2015's Council of Mortgage Lenders' figure indicate that well over 50 per cent of London dwelling properties are bought without mortgagees indicates the amount of cash, both personal and institutional, available to purchase property.[28] Whatever the (il)legality of that, the effect is further to inflate metropolitan property prices, dragging the lower tiers upwards.

Gentrification

Another factor contributing to rising house prices has been 'gentrification' – which has spread to many metropolitan areas. This is, in terms of design and fitment-quality, high-level refurbishment of previously overlooked areas. In London, Notting Hill, Shoreditch and Balham seem to be on every commentator's lists of sites of gentrification. Thanks to New York's influence, urban 'loft' developments are taking over many former industrial or warehouse units, such as Birmingham's Jewellery Quarter or Manchester's Market Street developments. Waterfront and canalside developments are another gentrifying mark of the past thirty years; Liverpool's Albert Dock complex, Birmingham and London's canalside developments and the media-complex-driven developments of Glasgow's Clyde, Leeds Aireside or Salford Quays are all prime nationwide examples. All these gentrified areas are becoming impervious to house-price dips.

Facing the Future

This chapter is a subjective essay; to treat any of its topics fully and objectively would have required its own chapter, if not a book. However, in attempting to offer a 'broad brush' history, greater attention has been given to those subjects which either may not be the experience of the general reader or are not covered in a later chapter by a specialist writer on those topics.

The development of Britain's housing has increased in its complexity. During the past century, the 'mix' of rental and owner-occupied properties has been vital in maintaining a just and equitable provision for most citizens. We need to note that this has not been true for *everyone*. The very fact that as this book goes to press, Parliament is continuing to debate the Homes (Fitness for Human Habitation) Bill shows that, in 2016, we have not learned the lessons of the past. Whether people are setting out as first-time householders by renting, or whether their lifestyle, by choice or through poverty, has not enabled them to climb onto the housing-ownership ladder, the need to ensure by statute that all landlords behave responsibly is an indictment of Britain today.

Well over 80 per cent of Britain's population live in urban areas, ranging from large cities with their dormitory areas to residential towns with more than fifteen thousand residents. Therefore, it is virtually impossible to provide similar 'broad brush' trends for changes in rural housing, except to say that the variety of need is vastly different, as Raymond Young indicates in Chapter 7, about rural provision.

As we read the subsequent chapters about different types of provision, we need to consider a whole variety of factors:

- The UK's current pattern of nuclear families and couples or singletons living in their own units is not universal.

- Could and should the common tradition in Mediterranean nations of multi-generational housing be enabled in Britain?

- Could and should the common north European practice of renting domestic homes – often within urban tenements, rural villages and dormitory towns, which allows more frequent 'upscaling' or 'downsizing' and thus more fluid and changing forms of social interaction and cohesion – be more justly facilitated in the UK?

- What does 'affordable' mean? How can rents and the provision of rental properties as well as house prices become affordable for lower paid people, to create housing justice as part of a sustainable society in which welfare and economic needs are met?

What is now evident, despite the complexity of both housing issues and the population's need, is that the Westminster Government does not share political consensus about the future trajectory for housing provision. I do not believe that it was simply post-war euphoria when Labour's Nye Bevan oversaw the introduction of fresh, major home-building initiatives in the 1946 and 1949 Housing Acts, which received cross-party support. Further, in the 1950s, the Conservative Harold Macmillan oversaw the building of nearly 300,000 homes in one calendar year. While doing that, Macmillan recalled Bevan's words, 'We shall be judged in one or two years by the quantity of houses we build, but in a decade we shall be judged upon the quality of houses that we build.'

Since then Britain has lost that sense of good political consensus, which then transcended party politics, for the common good. By late 2015, Chancellor Osborne's Spending Review made it clear that the responsibility for housing provision would be in the hands of private companies building homes, predominantly for purchase. To me, there is huge lack of realism in the Conservative Government offering their 20 per cent subsidies on homes costing £250,000 (or £450,000 in London) – these are totally unaffordable prices for the majority of people earning wages. Where is the Macmillan vision also to provide large numbers of dwellings at affordable rents?

The specialist writers of the following chapters document other changes which have led to the current dilemma about future housing provision. How much will Bevan's words come back to haunt us if wisdom does not prevail in the choices facing us all? This book, while learning lessons from our social history or contemporary European practices, seeks to use those writers' expertise to challenge our praxis – that is, both our action and our reflection.

Postscript
As stated in the Introduction, the editor implemented the 30 November 2015 cut-off date for the chapter contributors' written reflections. Since then, three significant events have occurred.

1. During the winter of 2015–16, an increased politicisation of the housing debate occurred. It was noticeable how increasingly politicians of the left (not just the Labour Party, but also the Greens and the SNP) used the phrase 'housing crisis'. This is an outworking of ongoing UK economic priorities as well as the failure to address the question of affordability for either tenants or purchasers. In marked contrast, the Conservative Government refrained from the term 'housing need' in favour of the expression 'housing situation', which, as Chancellor Osborne declared, requires 'more homes to be built' but without giving further reasoning. With the exception of the Greens and the SNP, most political rhetoric focused this debate upon London and the south east.

2. In early January 2016, Prime Minister Cameron announced that this year would see the government commission the building of 13,000 new homes, using £1.2bn of public money to kick-start this. This was in marked contrast to previous government expectation that private enterprise would kick-start the necessary house-building programme. However, it should be noted this government initiative was limited and spread across one site in London and four others in south-east England.

3. Then just a week later, this Prime Minister announced his government's intention to knock down and rebuild (low-rise) housing estates where poverty and social problems were rife.

   There's one issue that brings together many of these social problems . . . It's our housing estates . . . especially those built just after the war are actually entrenching poverty in Britain . . . and because poverty has become entrenched, because those who could afford to move have understandably done so.[29]

4. The mass media summarised it with headlines such as 'Cameron's plan to knock down tower blocks'. There was distinct absence of mention of any plans to deal with the inevitable mass relocation or the social dislocation to those communities and their local schools, shops and services. Have the Prime Minister or his advisers never read *Concretopia*, which advocates a more creative approach towards how brutalist architecture has shaped modern Britain?[30] Cameron was honest enough to say that he

preferred that the new homes would be affordable to purchase, rather than rent, but notably again without any definition of what 'affordable' practically means for the poorest sectors of society.

All this simply emphasises Britain's numerically growing 'housing need' as I perceive it. How that should and can be achieved within the means of all UK citizens, whether tenants or owners, regrettably remains unresolved.

Chapter Three

The Changing Role of the Local Authority in Housing Provision

Sean Gardiner

Everyone has the right to a standard of living adequate for the health and well-being of himself and of his family, including foods, clothing, housing and medical care and necessary social services, and the right to security in the event of unemployment, sickness, disability, widowhood, old age or other lack of livelihood in circumstances beyond his control.

Article 25 in the Universal Declaration of Human Rights

New housing estates – a dream smashed.

David Sheppard, Bias to the Poor

Among current specific issues to which the proclamation of Christian wholeness applies are education, housing, pollution, racism and unemployment.

Manifesto of Coalition for Urban Mission, 1981

My story starts with a quote from my wife: 'They say that your theology is shaped by where you sit ... So almost all the physical landscape I see ... is shaped for good or ill by decisions made in the political realm'.[1] She started life in a back-to-back terrace house in Sheffield. One of her earliest memories is the removal van taking her family to a new, system-built, concrete, council flat, as part of a 1960s slum clearance, so they could start a new life. In 1979 I started working in housing in Moss Side, Manchester, and we secured our first home, a freezing-cold private flat on the top floor of a Victorian house in Whalley Range, Manchester, the week before our marriage. I was made redundant in 1980 following the election of Margaret Thatcher's Conservatives, who cut financing for housing associations, and we then had five homes in our first two years together. I got a job in London and we moved only two weeks before the 1981 Moss Side riot, which we prophetically predicted to our very sceptical church before we left.

In 1983 we were homeless and were offered a thirteenth-floor tower-block flat by the Greater London Council and have happily lived there since, being part of the community, and raising two children, one of whom was born at home. The flat's ownership was transferred to Tower Hamlets Council and then to a housing association. We have remained tenants, always feeling the flat was gifted to us by the community and so we have not bought it even though it would make us a substantial personal profit – but we know many neighbours who bought theirs. Some have subsequently moved out and re-let their flats, some temporarily to the council for use by homeless people, who have to pay higher rents than we are charged. Most of the remaining tenants are those left behind without other options.

So how did we get to this point? In the nineteenth century the prevailing ethos about housing provision was that the market provided the housing people deserved, implying the poor were responsible for the squalid overcrowded conditions they lived in. The roots of council housing lie in three social movements which ran contrary to this ethos and are hinted at in the opening quotes. The first historically, and the most important, was the concern for public health and the need to provide a healthy environment for the working classes, which contributed to the model industrial villages and the garden city movement. Then Octavia Hill started a pioneering philanthropic housing management scheme with door-to-door rent collection, proper repairs and showing that when treated properly the poor could live decently. Social studies of the poor and poverty, often by early socialists, helped shift attitudes and so paved the way for state intervention in alleviating the housing conditions of the poor. These led to the 1890 Housing of the Working Classes Act, which empowered local authorities to clear slums and to keep and manage the new housing they built. The first council estate was London County Council's Boundary Street, Bethnal Green, replacing the Old Nichol slum. Some other cottage or tenement-design estates were built in London and other cities but, lacking a proper financial basis, were limited in number.

The unfit condition of many working-class recruits to the Boer War and World War I, with a wartime, private-rents freeze perpetuating the existing housing crisis, the building of state housing for war workers on garden-city lines, and the fear of rent strikes combining with industrial unrest culminated in Lloyd George's pledge to build 'habitations fit for the heroes who have won the war', more commonly cited as 'homes fit for heroes'. His Liberal Minister for Reconstruction, Dr Christopher Addison, was responsible for the 1919 Housing and Town Planning Act, keeping this role when he became Minister for Health. This made local authorities permanent suppliers of new, good-standard housing for working-class people, with a 75 per cent subsidy, plus all the costs exceeding the proceeds of a penny rate, and gave a subsidy for private building of housing for working-class people, but in the post-war situation this had very little take-up. The ministry's guidance on target rent levels was contradictory, aiming at different times to make an economic return, to be in line with local rents for working-class people, and to be affordable to those living there. The resulting rents were usually two or three times higher than private, frozen, pre-1914 rents, and rates were usually higher too, reflecting the better standards of the housing.[2] There were delays in starting building, the political consensus broke down and Addison was forced from office in 1921. His Act eventually resulted in 170,000 council homes being built and was the start of housing as a social service.

Since then the levels of the building of council housing, its rents, subsidies and management have all been subject to the political ideology of the ruling parties, with generally the Conservatives supporting building for private renting or owner-occupation and Labour supporting council housing, and latterly other forms of social housing, with Liberals making some key interventions through the twentieth century.

This see-saw started with the Conservative Neville Chamberlain's 1923 Housing Act, which reduced subsidies, giving only half the cost of any slum clearance, and lowered the quality of housing. The first and second Labour governments, 1924 and 1929–31, gave a larger subsidy to build council houses, and included measures for slum clearance and some properties with 'rent remission' to make them affordable to the poorest for the first time. The 1931–40 National Government ended the general subsidy for house-building. It encouraged slum clearance, but with little success except for some estates, mostly of tenement blocks, linked to the redevelopment of urban centres usually attached to road expansion.

Developments like Manchester's Wythenshawe were modelled on the garden-city ideal, with large council estates growing into small townships with the intention of building whole new communities but, as with so many estates before and after the World War II, the building of schools, shops, industrial buildings, churches and leisure facilities was delayed. Wythenshawe didn't reach its full size of 100,000 with a cinema, theatre, and a market until the 1970s. There were other experiments, notably Leeds' Quarry Hill estate, which was built using a prefabricated system with a French 'Garchey' waste-disposal system, lifts and other communal services.

The National Government's most significant contribution was probably allowing local authorities to pool rents and previous subsidies, which provided the basis for financing council housing. So from 1920 to 1939 about four million homes were built in Britain with one million of those being council housing. However, the quality of these homes varied considerably, depending on the resources available. At Trimdon in the Durham coalfield, they didn't replace the pitmen's cottages, which had communal standpipes and middens, until 1937. Jim Gregg, who was born in one, remembers: 'The council houses were terrible. They were in what they call the plantation and there were no proper streets, just rough dirt tracks.[3] At nearby Jarrow in 1938 the council built the Primrose estate with bathrooms, indoor WCs and upstairs bedrooms, but still with gas lights and a kitchen range.

By 1939 there was confusion about why council housing should be built. Was it to provide sanitary housing for the slum-dwellers, possibly freeing up some private rented stock for other poor? Or was it to provide housing for the poorest, with individual rebates; or for the better-paid working class people who could afford the rent; or for a more general clientele? This resulted in varying, often highly selective, allocation policies. Rent levels were variable even within each area and often in the same block so the vison was not clear to administrators or tenants.

After the 1939–45 wartime destruction, particularly in cities and industrial areas, accompanied by the lack of ordinary repair work, there was a huge demand for housing. It was also recognised, similar to the feeling in 1918, that after their service and sacrifice people had the right to expect a better quality of life. This culminated in the 1942 Beveridge Report, which named the social evils of squalor, ignorance, want, idleness and disease, and laid the basis for the welfare state. Beveridge's vision included a massive expansion of decent-standard council housing as part of the welfare state.

Housing was part of the remit of the Ministry of Health, so it came under the driving force and political direction of Aneurin Bevan. His large council estates, like the new garden towns, aspired to build whole new communities with housing for everyone. The estates were to be of different sizes and standards, all provided initially by local authorities. Bevan, now with Addison's support as Health Minister in the House of Lords, argued with the Treasury to limit the expected return from rents and to return to building council housing to the standards set in 1919. Bevan famously argued that 'while we shall be judged for a year or two by the *number* of houses we build . . . we shall be judged in ten years' time by the *type* of houses we build'. The three-bedroomed houses built then were on average 37 per cent larger than their pre-war equivalents and are still highly prized now.

The 1949 Housing Act had a vision for council housing to become a universal service available to all in need, not just the working class, aligning it with the vision and language of the new health service. From 1945 to 1951 a million new council homes were built, but even this did not meet the post-war housing need so from 1949 the government started to provide prefabricated homes, and adapted some previous military buildings to temporary housing.

Housing was celebrated as one of the post-war success stories, with the Lansbury estate in Poplar, East London, opening as part of the 1951 Festival of Britain. One of the original tenants, Sid Langley, later a church warden at All Saints Church, Poplar, recalls being proud to show visitors the good-quality flats and the cheap but fine furniture produced to equip them.[4]

The Conservative Harold Macmillan picked up this aspiration for a new home and launched a 'Great Housing Crusade', pledging to build 300,000 permanent new homes a year. He became the first Minister of Housing and continued to expand both the building industry and land available. In 1953 he celebrated the completion of the three-hundred-thousandth new home in the year, but two-thirds were provided by private developers with most going to owner-occupation, and to achieve this target he also deliberately reduced the expected standard of each home and permitted increased densities. Sid Langley, mentioned above, said in 1954: 'Our area had been the prime target of Hitler's Luftwaffe during the war, but they didn't do half the damage to us as Macmillan did with his so-called slum clearances!' Macmillan wanted the vision for council housing to shift to providing a temporary home until working tenants could afford to buy their own home.

During the 1950s the thinking behind designing council housing changed, following an example from Radburn, New Jersey, where cars and housing were kept separate. Houses were built in culs-de-sac or with separate rows of garages and play areas, both out of sight of the dwellings, so now leading to management problems. The paths and gardens looked inwards too so it could be hard to know which side was the front, signage was unclear, and shops or other communal facilities struggled to get established. In the 1950s and 1960s this planning philosophy was accompanied by technological improvements, so it led to deck access with long walkways or 'streets in the sky' replacing ground-level footpaths, with windswept communal areas of uncertain use surrounding them. Sheffield's Park Hill estate was an early example with most walkways leading to ground level, because of the hillside slope. The utopian village ideal lived on in this design, as in Leeds' Hunslet Grange estate with twelve hundred homes in four-deck-access 'village' blocks surrounding the open green, including shops and a pub. Overall though these flats, sometimes even surrounded by a boundary fence or wall, tend to be inward-looking, which separates estate residents from the wider community and makes it more difficult to attract outsiders in to use, and so make financially viable, estate shops and communal facilities.

In 1954 Macmillan announced that slum clearance would resume and in 1957 subsidy for general housing was ended. The local authorities were also encouraged to use the modern methods of prefabricated building systems, and to share in the Le Corbusier image of 'vertical cities'. To obtain maximum subsidies they built up to eleven floors, later increased to fifteen, but many authorities, under pressure to maximise land use, went up to twenty and in a few cases to thirty floors or more. Most estates had a mixture of high and low rise; often adjoining blocks were linked by walkways at different levels; and the 'pleasing' architectural variety and appearance was one of the factors leading to the growth of these estates, even in suburbs where the land cost did not make them the best option.

The quality of these new homes, though, was questioned and the government set up the Parker Morris commission to report on the design of their new modern homes. Their 1961 report, 'Homes for Today and Tomorrow', set mandatory standards for public-sector housing from 1961 (until it was abolished by Margaret Thatcher's government in 1981). This set generous space standards and ended prescriptive advice on room arrangements; instead it recommended multi-use of rooms during the day, and possibly changing use during the building's life, facilitated by central heating and more electrical sockets.

To meet the promise of fast-to-build, cheap, high-quality modern buildings, there was a coming together of those anxious to clear the slums and provide modern cities. People from all political parties in central and local government, developers, large construction companies with all the associated professionals, town planners, environmental health officers and architects were all attracted to the larger cities and established lucrative, mutually supportive arrangements. These culminated in 1974 in the conviction of T. Dan Smith, 'Mr Newcastle', for corruption, and of John Poulson, leader of a large architectural practice, for fraud.

Through this whole period the press generally announced new housing provision as part of 'you've never had it so good' or even from the left as progressive and modern. The largely missing voice was that of the residents; those I have included from this period were positive about their new homes, but by the 1970s there were dissenting voices.

John Bage in South Shields lived in a council flat provided for shipyard workers. It comprised a scullery, one living room and one bedroom, but after his parents had their third child in 1957 they moved to a new, three-bedroom, terraced council house in Whiteleas estate outside the town. He recalls: 'When we moved to this other place where there was fields and grass and freedom and space, what a difference it made to our lives . . . We used to . . . wander across the fields and go to local farms. In that house we had a bath with hot and cold water. It was amazing. We had an upstairs and a downstairs and a front garden and a back garden to play in. Incredible.'[5] Others who benefited from the slum clearance welcomed moving into new homes on inner-city estates, as I have been told by some of the first residents of Broadwater Farm and Hulme estates.

However, there were concerns about the quality of life in high-rise buildings, and in 1967 the Labour government ended their subsidy. In 1968 a 22-storey block at Ronan Point, Newham, partially collapsed following a small gas explosion, and four people died. Building other blocks was paused; some local authorities added strengthening and some banned gas supplies.

The council building of high-rise flats ended. They were only about 2 per cent of all council homes but they were noticeably concentrated and in some London boroughs provided almost half their stock. They produced some of the iconic image of council estates, such as Glasgow's Gorbals, with 208 blocks, or Manchester's Hulme Crescents. Birmingham tried to disperse their 463 tower blocks around the city but overall had possibly the highest concentration.

After this, council housing building slowed through the 1970s and was brought almost to a standstill after the 1977 oil price crisis and the pressure on public finances. The Labour government publicly accepted the aspiration for owner-occupation, and available resources were switched to repairs and the maintenance of existing housing. In 1977 the Liberal, David Steel, with Labour support, guided the Homeless Persons Act through Parliament, giving local authorities the duty to house homeless families and the elderly or otherwise vulnerable people. Since that time, the allocation of council housing has, in many urban authorities particularly, become a struggle to meet this demand above all others and to provide temporary accommodation until these families are housed.

The 1979 Conservative government introduced the right for council tenants to buy their homes at substantial discounts. Many became homeowners for the first time, and when they later sold the houses they made a substantial profit, which some used to start businesses. It was claimed this gave them a new sense of pride. However, as one who has lived and worked among those left behind, I am convinced there are significant issues. The government did not fund the discount and add it to the capital receipt and make this available to provide a replacement. These properties were partly funded from the exchequer, which is made up of contributions from everyone, and partly by borrowing funded by pooled rent paid by all tenants. The fortunate person who happens to buy their home at a discount makes a personal profit but removes it from the stock available to house others. Many of these are later relet to a succession of short-term private tenancies, often leading to problems for their neighbours.

There is often comparatively little said about how council housing is managed. Management has oscillated between being provided by locally based teams dealing with all issues, or from a central 'town hall' base, often split into specialist and apparently more cost-effective teams. I managed the team at Broadwater Farm Neighbourhood Office in Tottenham, Haringey, from 1989. The office had been set up in response to residents' demands in 1983, and had led the responses to the 1985 riot. We knew many tenants personally, ensuring we carried out repairs and dealt with tenants' issues promptly, while they paid their rent. Meanwhile we worked with the Priority Estates Project (PEP) to reform the residents' association and, with a succession of local leaders, to turn the estate around after the riot. PEP's advocacy for and work on challenging estates is reminiscent of Octavia Hill's work to humanise and personalise the housing service for a deprived community. The estate benefited from several Christians deliberately moving onto the estate to work with residents to help bring hope and a sense of a positive future to the community We attracted different funding streams, notably £33 million of estate action funding to knock down walkways, install concierge-controlled door-entry schemes, provide external thermal cladding and change the oil-fired district heating to mainly gas central heating.

The 1997 Labour government concentrated its housing budget on the massive backlog of improvement to bring council homes, which had been mainly starved of resources from 1979 to 1997 up to a new standard, defined as the Decent Homes standard. They supported replacing monolithic council housing departments by encouraging stock transfers. Some councils sold or transferred all their stock to existing housing associations, or set up new housing associations, or new Arm's Length Management Organisations, which managed properties while retaining council ownership, as in Haringey, while in Tower Hamlets each estate had a choice of transferring to a choice of housing associations or staying with their ALMO.

In 2011, Mark Duggan, a previous resident of the Broadwater Farm estate, was shot by the police. This led to a riot, not on the estate itself, but on Tottenham High Road, and the pattern spread around the country. As so often following a riot, there are now new resources and a new vision for Tottenham, including efforts to reach out to include the disaffected. However, Broadwater Farm Neighbourhood Office was comparatively expensive to run and so was closed in 2013. Under the current austerity drive, housing and other public services are provided in fewer locations, with staff specialisations, and increasing use of telephone and online services to reduce the expensive personal interaction with tenants.

Since 2013 I have managed Homes for Haringey's new Financial Inclusion Team, helping tenants meet the challenges of the bedroom tax, benefit cap, demands that adult children living with tenants make increasing rent contributions and effects of benefit sanctions. Tenants are facing further cuts as the levels of the benefit cap is reduced and other benefits are likely to be at a standstill in coming years. Monthly universal credit payments given to council tenants themselves will replace housing benefit that was paid directly into their rent accounts. This will be a major budgeting challenge as many tenants will receive more money than ever before but will have to spread it over a month, including rent. There is a substantial risk that rent arrears will grow, causing further pressure on council housing finances.

The popular image of an underclass on council estates involved in street culture, drugs, loud music and violence is only part of the life and experience of these estates, and lacks analysis of relationships and life chances for young people growing on these estates. All these features were mentioned in a *London Evening Standard* series published on 28–30 September 2015 about the Angell estate near Elephant and Castle, but typically were not carried through into the articles on the next page, analysing the effects of increasing house prices in London on 28 September, or reducing the number of police community officers on 29 September, respectively.

The new Conservative government seems to be leaving the Beveridge vision of council housing provision for all and going back to Macmillan's vision of councils providing only a temporary home until working tenants could afford to buy their own home. Since their election they have proposed to extend the right to buy to housing association properties, many of which were built by charities and with a mixture of funding. They will force councils to sell their most valuable properties to fund this. To their credit, housing associations have been reluctant to accept this scheme whereby two homes are removed from the supply of properties available (for those in temporary accommodation or those who will be homeless in the future), with a hope that one replacement will be provided later. It provides profit for one household but at a cost to the whole community – and like an Old Testament prophet we need to question this.

The government also proposes reducing social rents by 1 per cent per annum, which is designed to cut the housing benefit bill regardless of the effect on social housing budgets. They also propose making higher-earning tenants pay commercial rents, and to end council housing being offered as permanent homes and instead to provide for only temporary tenancies. Under the cover of austerity, these measures are reworking the debates on the proper level of rents, how tenants should be supported, and the vision of the purpose of council housing. Is it a residual service only for the homeless? When people are working should they buy their property or be forced out into the private sector, or could council housing still be an arm of the welfare state providing housing for all? Council housing has been a valuable resource provided by everyone over the last century to provide decent housing for those in need. Christians in particular should appreciate that pooling our resources to provide for those in need (as in Acts 2) is a responsibility of the whole society, and that housing is about people and communities – not just bricks, mortar and money.

Chapter 4

The Development of Housing Associations

Chris Horton

Housing associations are, in the words of a leading housing lawyer, 'curious entities', because they are neither private trading bodies driven by a profit motive, nor democratically elected public bodies, nor government appointed bodies.[1] They are technically private bodies so their borrowings are not on the public-sector balance sheet, yet they are for community or charitable purposes.[2] Many have received public subsidies (grant to develop properties or low-cost land) and are required to act as public bodies for many purposes by the housing regulator, yet their current legal title is *private* registered providers. The majority are exempt charities or registered charities, yet most do not fit the popular image of a charity. They sit awkwardly between the three sectors of private, public and voluntary, yet they own around 2.3 million of the 4.1 million affordable housing properties in England.

The housing association sector seems diverse, with some associations specialising in certain types of tenants or service users (e.g. learning disabled, ex-offenders, elderly), and most operate only in certain geographical locations. Some are large. Places for People owns or manages around 150,000 units (half as much again as its nearest rival) and has reported aspirations to become listed on the London Stock Exchange.[3] Most of the 1,783 'registered providers' in England are relatively small, with 5,000 being typical and the smallest owning only a handful of units of housing in one scheme.[4]

The influence of the housing regulators, however, has tended toward homogeneity since the mid-1970s.[4] Viewed from the present, the various steps in the history of housing associations might seem to lead clearly and logically to their current pattern. On this assumption, the only real challenge is to identify the time from which the current pattern is recognisable, and the 1988 Housing Act seems to mark such a boundary between 'then' and 'now'. It laid the legislative foundations for a period of dramatic growth of the housing association sector, while at the same time raising private finance became the single most important factor in that growth. This innovation in financing social housing was achieved for the first time in May 1987 by Home HA.[6] It was made possible by the grant regime administered by the Housing Corporation after the 1974 Housing Act, which seems, with hindsight, to be the essential prior step. We can trace many prior steps of course.

This is too simplistic an approach, however, as there was a great deal of thought and activity, particularly from the 1860s onwards, that could have led the sector in a very different direction or multiple directions at once. Furthermore, a simple pre- or post-1988 boundary fails to do justice to the complex history of almshouses, co-operatives, industrial societies, local redevelopment companies and philanthropic charities. Not only were there different types of organisation with varying emphases, there was a degree of conflict in aims and methods among them and conflicts with central and local government too, often with a political dimension.

It would, again, be simplistic to suggest that it all goes back to the year 1235. But that is when St Lawrence's Hospital Charity was formed. It is the oldest member of the National Housing Federation, the representative, lobbying and advisory body for housing associations, which itself was formed seven hundred years later in 1935. St Lawrence's was endowed for the benefit of two female lepers in Cirencester and stands in the medieval tradition of wealthy benefactors fulfilling their religious duties to those less well off (particularly lepers, pilgrims, disabled and poor).[7] They often hoped their charitable acts would be recognised in heaven and the provision often went far beyond mere housing.[8] Almshouses and hospitals alike were inspired by the work of monasteries and it is therefore not possible to identify a particular origin for the provision of charitable housing for those in need.

The Reformation closed the monasteries but not the monastic hospitals and did not stop the flow of funds, even if the precise form of the motivation may have changed. In the early seventeenth century there was a great increase in the number of almshouses. A wealthy merchant was expected by the community at large to endow charitable works.[9] And for those whose motives were mixed, what could be better than a building, a permanent memorial of their charity and piety?

Almshouses continued to be endowed in the nineteenth century, and over 30 per cent of existing almshouses come from that century, but they were inadequate for the numbers of working, able-bodied poor living in urban centres following the Industrial Revolution.[10]

More creative solutions, motivated by a variety of impulses, had to be attempted and, as the housing was needed for those who could pay rent within limits, rather than depend on charity, there was scope for provision without major subsidy.

The description 'philanthropy at 5 per cent' came into use in 1887 to describe a number of different bodies set up from about 1830. The investor's return on capital in the form of dividends was limited 'in order to provide accommodation on terms that were affordable to their intended working-class tenants'.[11] Instead of normal levels of dividends at 7 per cent to 10 per cent, a return limited to 5 per cent satisfied the investor's philanthropic motivation while still providing a decent return on investment. It avoided undermining the accepted social order. Typically these companies, funded by the investments of wealthy individuals, were 'model dwellings companies' that produced buildings to a standard, i.e. a model that could be easily copied. In London, where the first were active, they tended to be tenement blocks: the high value of land forced compromises in achieving the aims of quality accommodation at affordable rents.

At the same time there were charitable trusts, companies with similar aims of housing the working, urban poor, but whose benefactors endowed them with capital. The rate of return expected was lower for charities and, for example, the Peabody Donation Fund sought 3 per cent while the Guinness Trust's target was 3.5 per cent. George Peabody, an American banker resident in London, endowed the first major model dwellings company in 1862 and has been seen by some as the father of modern philanthropy. However, even with some land acquisitions from the local government at a reduced price, by the end of the century the Peabody Trust was housing more of the better-off working-class people than the poor originally envisaged as its tenants; like all these providers the Peabody Trust needed sufficient rental income to cover the costs of building, management and repair.

Another strand was the co-operative societies. In the late eighteenth century, Birmingham's rapid growth prompted the first co-operative building societies where pooled savings enable members to build their own houses. Although these societies had usually been intended to close down once all members were housed, they often became financial savings and lending institutions that flourished from the late nineteenth century. But there were a number of experiments in different ways of co-operating, only some of which were allied to the political and social movement comprising co-operative societies.

Sometimes they pooled finance, sometimes they pooled labour and often the society retained ownership but let the properties to members. The prime example of lettings was the type of co-partnership housing societies led and promoted from 1890 by Henry Vivian, later a Liberal MP. Tenants were required to be shareholders, but investment was open to others and these financiers soon came to dominate the societies. Nevertheless this model was employed successfully in the early 1900s to develop many of the over-fifty garden suburbs in England.

Among the garden suburbs were those developed by wealthy industrialists to 'ameliorate the conditions of the labouring classes'.[12] Lever's model village at Port Sunlight was, like previous employer-built villages, aimed at a happy and productive workforce. But the Quaker chocolate magnates Cadbury and Rowntree were more far-sighted and laid more of a foundation for the later housing associations. A rate of return was required to ensure sustainability (4 per cent in the Cadbury case at Bourneville); the design was intended to improve upon the typical municipal council layouts and properties were not exclusively for employees.

Perhaps the most famous forerunner is Octavia Hill. She pioneered housing management from 1865 with determination to link idealism (she was strongly influenced by F.D. Maurice and the Christian Socialists) with pragmatic and practical applications. She wrote movingly of the crowded and unhealthy conditions of the urban poor but her contribution was to show how active management, with personal contact, could enable landlords and volunteers to enable the poor to help themselves. This was more than social work. Though personal contact was seen as redemptive, and outings for children and social events were part of rescuing the poor from dissolute ways, her method was business-like. Landlords would get a 5 per cent return and had to be responsible in carrying out repairs in return for rents. Hill's energies extended to being a founder of the National Trust, and her links with Ruskin (for whom she managed properties) also indicate the holistic philosophical approach: the preservation of a common heritage and pursuit of beauty linked very closely with education and decent conditions for the poor. Tenants needed to be treated well so they could contribute well. She wrote: 'The fulfilment of their duties was the best education for the tenants in every way. It has given them a dignity and glad feeling of honourable behaviour which has much more than compensated for the apparent harshness of the rule.'[13]

Historians often point to the relatively low numbers of dwellings actually constructed by these bodies, and their poor design by later standards, as a failure that led inevitably to state intervention. Malpass doubts both that they failed and that intervention was inevitable.[14] The problem of migrant workers from rural areas and other parts (particularly Ireland) was on a massive scale, however, and by 1891 the thirty or so companies and trusts active in London were housing 72,000 people, which was little more than the *annual* increase in London's population.[15] Though they had not proved that the market, with help of low-rate capital or endowments, could solve the housing crisis on a large scale, they succeeded at least in experimenting with various creative solutions.

In the diverse movement many of the model dwelling companies targeted the poor in a way that appealed to conservative, wealthy benefactors and philanthropists. Co-partnership was more progressive politically and 'bottom-up' in approach. Octavia Hill's management methods were perhaps patronising by today's standards but a genuine attempt to help people improve their lot. Some co-operative societies were part of a radical political movement and some of the garden cities aimed at a utopian future. There was no shared identity and as World War I loomed it became clear that none of these models could 'overcome the central problem of how to generate sufficient capital to make a significant impact on the housing shortage without sacrificing quality or affordability'.[16]

Following World War I, the government was compelled by a number of factors to subsidise 'homes fit for heroes', but the private and co-operative or charitable developers remained unable to build on the scale needed. The 1919 Housing and Town Planning Act did give councils the power to assist voluntary housing bodies with grants and loans, though examples are few.[17] The councils intentionally targeted the working classes rather than the poor, in contrast to the main aims of the voluntary societies, the most vibrant of which operated on Octavia Hill's principles of middle-class outreach to the poor in the slums.[18]

Debate continued on how best to provide social housing, and the 1935 Moyne Committee's proposals would have given associations a greater role, but the subsequent 1935 Housing Act left local authorities dominant for fifty years. Associations continued to raise finance and do local deals to improve certain areas on a relatively small scale. But councils tended to be hostile. Conservatives saw them as unable to operate on the necessary scale and Labour politicians were unsympathetic to unaccountable associations, largely run by upper- and middle-class people suspected of Tory leanings.

In the early 1960s, housing association activity increased, largely due to promotional efforts by various church-based groups and some support from the Greater London Council and certain other councils.[19] By 1974, the sector was completing nearly ten thousand dwellings per annum compared with nearly three thousand in 1964 but it was still a drop in the ocean. The 1974 Housing Act transformed this in response to a growing consensus that gradual renewal was better than large-scale redevelopment and that some variety in ownership of rented housing was valuable (though the preference for council housing among Labour politicians remained strong and widespread). The Act introduced a housing association grant and loan finance, together with fair rents, giving housing associations the luxury of a risk-free environment. It lasted only to 1988 but allowed the sector to become established as a credible alternative, and in 1980 nearly 39,000 dwellings were completed by housing associations. This security came at a cost, of course, in losing the diversity in structures and approaches. Associations were also seen as part of the public sector, which was a disadvantage in surrendering control (accepting the government's design standards and other conditions of grant) but an advantage in overcoming some of the Labour Party's hostility to social housing being provided by any entity other than councils.

The Housing Corporation had been established in 1964 but in the 1974 Act was given a wide role as regulator. The corporation increasingly became a means of the government imposing its policy choices on associations, and 'policy passporting' remained a very significant influence on the sector until the demise of the Housing Corporation in 2008. During the 1980s, the corporation used its funding conditions to direct associations towards refurbishment and provision for the elderly, rather than towards new building. More subtle influences included pressure to recruit development staff rather than rely upon consultants, and excluding board members who had a financial interest in the association.[20] Generally, associations became more homogeneous in the way they operated.

The Thatcher government also tried to impose the 'right to buy' on housing associations but this was resisted by the National Federation's allies in the House of Lords. Eventually in 1984 tenants acquired the right to acquire at a modest discount. Although this is reimbursed to housing associations, the loss of stock can still be damaging to business and estate planning. However, the most significant change was the shift to private finance and the 1988 Housing Act provided the legislative framework for this in a way that has not been overturned. The Blair government's 2008 Housing and Regeneration Act promised a major change in the basis of council and association provision and their regulation, but in fact did little to alter the policy direction.[21]

The third Conservative election victory in 1987 on the back of economic boom enabled Margaret Thatcher to implement a lasting shift in the political landscape. The move to monetarist economic policy in the early 1980s was now followed by a renewed reduction in the public sector, with privatisation as a key policy. The 'right to buy' initiative had done much to create the desired 'property-owning democracy' and the government needed to continue the momentum in housing policy while recognising the need to make some provision for those who would not be able to buy their own property and could not afford market rents. The government could not rely merely on the private sector to provide enough rented accommodation and would not for political reasons rely on the local authorities to do so. Some damaging consequences of this change of policy have been described in Chapter 3.

The direction was set by a White Paper in 1987 which stated: 'The future role of local authorities will essentially be a strategic one identifying housing needs and demands, encouraging innovative methods of provision by other bodies to meet such needs, maximising the use of private finance, and encouraging the new interest in the revival of the independent rented sector.'[22] So councils were to move away from housing provision towards enabling other bodies to provide it. Investment in private renting was to be encouraged by removing security of tenure and rent control altogether. And private finance was to be brought into housing associations.

The 1988 Housing Act provided a new framework for associations and included machinery for tenants to choose to opt out of the local authority sector and transfer to a new landlord. Further, a local government Act the following year restricted council finances in relation to housing dramatically. Private-sector rents and supply increased very quickly but fewer than one thousand properties transferred from local authorities until further legislation in 1996 enacted new legal machinery to bring about the desired transfer of tenancies to housing associations from councils.

The Housing Corporation reduced the proportion of a development it would finance – a beneficial effect on the public finances – but the availability of loan finance enabled the sector to raise £11.4 billion for development and refurbishment by 1998, even before the bulk of the large-scale voluntary transfers that saw around half of the local authority dwellings move to the 'private sector'. Housing associations began to look and act more like commercial bodies. For example, most boosted their newly important finance functions, to cope with Treasury management and the long-term business plans required to prove to the banks that their loans would be repaid in due course. The influence of the banks' requirements was another factor in making associations more homogeneous.

Following 1988, the government exerted greater control over associations through the Housing Corporation; the amount of grant and the assumptions in the grant model became highly influential and the threat (whether implicit or explicit) of enforcement action made the 'guidance' of the regulator very persuasive! It is interesting to note, however, that, despite the growing homogeneity noted above, there is a distinction in governance between transfer vehicles and traditional housing associations. Typically, new bodies have been established for transfers; this has been read as implied criticism of the lack of local accountability in traditional associations.[23] Appointment of board members is exclusively by the existing board in traditional associations whereas councils typically have some 'golden share' rights in transfers, including a right to appoint one or more directors.

Governance is about more than how directors are appointed and includes the culture of an organisation. Christians have always played a major role in the voluntary sector and provided the impetus to establish many housing associations. A Christian ethos is hard to maintain, however, when the regulator pressurises associations in various ways to implement government policy, and the natural changes over time mean staff with very different belief systems are brought in. Further, a Christian foundation is no guarantee of quality.

The Audit Commission report in 2003 into Shaftesbury Housing, for example, found this organisation with a Christian ethos failed not just in compliance with the regulator's agenda prompted by the government's policy, but also in the basics of managing tenancies.[24] Even worse, a re-inspection the following year found no real improvement, though a new executive team was working hard to make significant changes.[25] It is disappointing to see an organisation –recognised as having many good employees trying to do the right thing – fail because its systems and processes are inadequate. It is particularly disappointing to see an organisation with a Christian origin fail when our theological framework is informed by such statements as 'You are the light of the world. A city set on a hill cannot be hidden.'[26] If the church is to be light as Jesus is, then we should, of all people, be the best at bringing together and managing teams to be effective. Our theology and faith should prompt us, more effectively than any pressure from the government, to work hard to make communities and the lives of tenants better.

Human existence outside the *shalom* of God is subject to the principle of entropy – everything is in decay.[27] In the social housing sector there seems to be a tendency towards decline from lofty ambitions to transform slums to commercial 'realities'. Many organisations were founded by well-meaning philanthropists or Christians fired with vision and compassion for God's will to be done 'on earth as it is in heaven'. Often they have developed into companies with the same culture and business practices as any private business.[28]

So this brief survey of the history of associations raises some obvious questions. Is it realistic to expect associations to keep true to their values while 'playing the game' according to the rules the regulator prescribes? Should we accept that the role of the church is merely to start something that would not otherwise start and to be glad that others take it on and take control of it? Or should we seek to be prophetic and not accept all the benefits and costs of receiving grant funding (including complying with 'policy passporting' through the regulators)? If the answer to the last question is affirmative then are we Christians willing to demonstrate a spiritual approach to governance that is even better than that prescribed by the regulator?

Chapter Five

The Changing City Landscape

Helen Roe

This chapter focuses mainly on London – where London leads, other cities often follow. In recent years residents will have observed many changes to this flexible city. The settings for familiar landmarks are changing, some disappearing. Buildings are being expanded, refaced. Banks have become restaurants, offices, houses and retail outlets. Many post offices have closed, replacements in the form of shops or cafés with post offices attached have slipped onto the streets. Doctors' surgeries are expanding; consequentially some are not so local. Urban petrol stations are being replaced with flats or houses. Public houses have been turned into showrooms, restaurants, shops selling mirrors. Small shops have become offices or residential properties. Flats pop up in place of single-storey buildings, and empty buildings are demolished to make way for houses. Office blocks are rapidly becoming flats under 'permitted development' rules which will continue indefinitely beyond May 2016, and residential properties are international investments as well as homes.

Internet shopping convenience means increasing numbers of local London areas have seen the loss of unviable (but maybe very useful) local shops, and their replacement with coffee bars and a plethora of cafés and restaurants, reflecting London's multicultural and diverse constituency. Shopping has long been at the heart of place-making, but active city centres and large stores have fought back, investing and upgrading so that visitors become customers who purposefully come to enjoy the shopping experience, linger and return for more. Customer service becomes important. The expansion of universities and accompanying rise of large-scale student housing local to their campuses brings students who relate to their university, not necessarily the locality beyond the convenience store.

At the same time in other parts of this dynamic city, and in response to the constant demand for housing in quality spaces, some brownfield sites have been developed that embrace the changes to shopping and working habits. Each has its own unique sense of neighbourhood and city buzz. The Department for Communities and Local Government gives the definition of brownfield sites as 'Previously developed land which is or was occupied by a permanent structure, including the curtilage of the developed land and any associated fixed surface infrastructure.'

Due to the significance of brownfield development in London, this chapter will explore three different approaches to its challenge and opportunities. All these schemes are being undertaken in close collaboration with the local authority and surrounding communities.

The Queen Elizabeth Olympic Park must surely be the nation's most well-known, former brownfield site. The promise of a 2012 Olympic legacy permanently to transform this former industrial area shared by four London boroughs and also to invigorate the lives of East Londoners played a significant part in the success of the London Olympic bid. The London Organising Committee for the Olympic Games (LOCOG) was committed to the rebirth of this area, of small-scale industrial units and older rundown industrial land, wasteland and unused space. Because its western edge was bordered by a toxic canal, with equally polluted rivers running through the site, there were a great many brownfield challenges facing the successful LOCOG in July 2005.

The Guardian's report in February 2012 headlined that the Olympic site had been certified clean – which meant that an area the size of 297 football pitches, much of which had previously been polluted, had successfully been cleaned. Invasive species of Japanese knotweed, Himalayan balsam and floating pennywort had been removed from the rivers, along with concrete walls, to improve the riverine habitat for wildlife and users. Three hundred thousand wetland plants, three thousand native trees and five miles of the River Lea had been restored. The Environment Agency decontaminated 2 million tonnes of soil for further use. Waste water is now reused, and the recycling plant and energy centre produces enough low-carbon energy to power ten thousand homes. Over twenty miles of cycleways and footpaths were laid and Britain's largest urban park for over a century was created, rescued from contaminated industrial land.[1]

Annual milestones have been put in place with quarterly reporting updates to achieve the promised ten-year plan up to March 2023.[2] Its stated targets include exemplary waste management including zero waste from short-term events going to landfill and ongoing financial sustainability by creating thirteen thousand new jobs through developments in the park.[3] Commercially, Here East (the former press and broadcasting hub which will become a new digital quarter with commercial space providing 7,500 jobs on site and in the local community) and Olympicopolis have been developed to become the new university and cultural quarter. The park aims to operate on a stable financial footing without public subsidy and to ensure the Paralympic legacy continues.

Economic recovery and cultural participation will ensure local people benefit from the success of the Queen Elizabeth Olympic Park and continued connections will support surrounding thriving town centres. A commitment to deliver the first 2,500 homes in the park and two quality new schools is on track.

Major employers are already signing up for the high-quality office spaces, drawn by the current shortage of this level of new accommodation in the West End or Canary Wharf. To date Transport for London and the Financial Conduct Authority have already committed themselves, along with University College London for a UCL East, a new University of the Arts London campus, Sadler's Wells, and the Victoria and Albert Museum. Securing employment in this area is key to its continuing development and sustainability.

The Mayor of London also published the Olympic Legacy Supplementary Planning Guidance document,[4] which sets out the long-term vision for the park and surrounding area, acknowledging that this will be London's most important regeneration project over the next twenty years and will sustain existing communities, promote local economic investment to create job opportunities – especially for young people – and should be driven by community engagement. The document sets out a continuation of the Olympic precedents of high-quality building design; environmental design; waste management; existing and new housing; and social, community and cultural infrastructure so that the areas around will continue to benefit. There will be a further, selectively managed release of appropriate industrial sites for mixed-use developments, to be carried out to the original Olympic Games standards.

Container City Live–Work Units

The subject of the second study is Container City, Trinity Buoy Wharf, Leamouth, East London, opposite the O2 arena on the other side of the River Thames. This example of transforming a brownfield site could not be more different in both scale and resources. Container City was the brainchild of Eric Reynold's Urban Space Management.

Eric Reynolds is the visionary who has already created some of London's most well-known and loved destinations from former run-down, often brownfield sites. Probably at the top of this list would be the transformation of Camden Lock in North London, once a derelict canal zone which he could see had the potential to become a 'happening place'. By inviting artists and setting up a craft market, which sold Peruvian wool gloves and products made by the craftspeople, he drew people to the area, which became a destination for the cultural taste of browsing and buying original craft or art items and street food from around the world also sold from stalls. Dingwall's rock venue brought in musicians. Restaurants established household names here, for example, the Camden Brasserie. The trendy Kings Road and Carnaby Street had been replaced. Camden Lock was on the map and the value of nearby residential properties increased.

Reynolds brings a wide understanding of the needs of London city-dwellers to regenerating brownfield sites by providing attractive places at low cost. No stranger to 'making things happen', his wide and creative remit in the past has included churches in shopping centres, museums in cottages, theatres in industrial buildings, an opera house, swimming pools, offices, pubs, art galleries, schools, markets, stations, a telephone exchange, a lighthouse, and working with Gravesend when that town suffering from the effects of the Bluewater Shopping Centre which opened nearby.

Urban Space Management[5] won the masterplan commission from London Docklands Development Corporation (LDDC). At the cost of £1.00, a 120-year lease to Trinity Buoy Wharf Trust (TBWT) was granted on the basis of the wharf being used for creative and artistic purposes. Under this deal TBWT pays a fixed 25 per cent of whatever they earn each year to the LDDC, who favoured this option over the established city developers' proposals. Reynolds used his connections with artists to kick-start a community scheme. He is quoted as saying, 'Artists are braver than most of us. Where they go, others follow.'[6] He had proved this before. Reynolds' mission is to 'tread lightly on the soil, leave others to be involved creatively and recycle hard'.

Two 40- to 50-square-metre insulated containers with windows cut into the sides and doors installed at one end provide a reasonable habitable space with kitchen, work and sleep areas, shower room and relaxation space. The containers, which were built with the help of an architect and a structural engineer, are stacked colourfully four storeys high and are now home to around seventy creative people. As well as sculptors and artists, musicians in residence have been known to bring out their violins in the evening and to play together, joined by other residential creatives. A small, colourful, children's nursery nestles alongside a foliage-covered container café; an American diner offers fast food; there is an outdoor performance space along with outdoor sculptures in every corner. Creativity abounds. Reynolds envisaged a people's park for those who want to make their place a home, not just somewhere to eat and sleep. Creatives often have to deal with poverty, loneliness and isolation; this type of development at £40 per week for some is an answer.

This vibrant mixed-use wharf currently has three different groups of container live-work studios. One of these, Clipper House, a four-storey container building is the relocated and reconfigured BBC Outside Broadcasting container studio formerly used in the Olympics and now home to the Princes Drawing School, part of the University of East London and the Thames Clipper headquarters. City firms hire spaces for entertainment, and English National Opera store their containers on site while their lorry parking is located nearby.

Live–Work Units in Hackney and Shoreditch[7]
Another form of live–work units briefly existed in the East End. In the battle to retain employment in its area, the London Borough of Hackney moved towards permitting people to live in long-term vacant properties unsuitable for general residential on the top floors of vacant industrial units. Chronic oversupply of empty industrial buildings led to adoption of this live–work policy supported by Hackney as a means of establishing small businesses and a legitimate way of responding to the 'new ways of working' initiative, bringing mixed use and employment, sustainable development and revitalisation to dead areas, by re-activating vacant buildings and enhancing conservation areas.

To meet live–work criteria, the minimum size of unit had to be 70 square metres – although in practice some were substantially larger. A functional workspace to accommodate office or work uses (B1 planning classification) had to be identified and 2-metre-wide entrance doors incorporated. These units were not generally permitted on the ground floor. Often known as 'lofts' or studios, they initially attracted artists, photographers, designers, craftspeople in ceramics, wood and glass, small-scale architects and the people in fashion trade. Hackney became established as the home of 'Brit Art' in the 1990s.

Live–work encouraged self-employed initiative-takers and small businesses into the borough. Hackney also received applications to introduce residential premises into small-scale commercial units. Live–work had become a familiar term.

Commercial developers quickly identified the desirability of reusing historical buildings to provide unusual, high-ceilinged residential accommodation with open-plan layouts, without having to meet statutory requirements for social housing provision. Planning approvals were given on the basis that both living and work spaces were to be provided – in reality they became pure residential buildings, subject to council-tax payments, but with no requirement to pay business rates on the 'work' element of the unit. After four years, established-use rights would secure their designation as residential.

The London Borough of Hackney finally followed Tower Hamlets and Islington in abolishing the planning term of the live–work hybrid as it had become a loophole for developers and commercial gain, but the terminology and vision for local work and living spaces within the city lives on.

Developer-Led Changes to Brownfield Sites

The third study is the well-known example of an ongoing project to bring the former Kings Cross goods yards and sidings into a first-choice destination for living, working and recreation. As with the Olympic Park, many aspects of this brownfield site have been developed to provide an enriching experience for those who are fortunate enough to live or work there, for visitors and also those passing through.

The Kings Cross development site was an important industrial heartland between the Kings Cross and St Pancras railway stations, stretching northwards into former railway sidings, sheds and Victorian stores. By the latter part of the last century, this vast area had become a dark piece of urban wasteland, disused buildings, unappreciated warehouses and desolate railway sidings. This contaminated land and the surrounding area of Kings Cross had acquired a reputation for shady drug-dealing and street-walking prostitution. At night it was becoming a 'no go' area.[8]

The decision, in 1996, to move Channel Tunnel Rail Link access to St Pancras became the catalyst for change. In 2001, Argent was selected as the preferred development partner by the landowners, Excel, and London and Continental Railways. The project began with several years of extensive studies and consultation with the local community, local authorities, government and other stakeholders to agree the basis of the redevelopment vision.

Workshops held by Argent and the three master planning-design offices resulted in Argent's vision for Kings Cross, 'Principles for a Human City', published in 2001,[9] recognised the value of providing a place for longevity with a vibrant mix of uses, promoting accessibility, harnessing the value of heritage and to be engaging and inspiring. It aimed at restoring pride into working at Kings Cross, London, and being committed to long-term success by securing the delivery and a successful completion. Open and clear communications were seen as imperative to ensure support along the way.

Argent estimated that 45,000 people a day will benefit from the 316,000 square metres of office space, 46,400 square metres for retail and leisure, and almost 2,000 homes. Their vision was to create a scheme which would be part of London, a busy place with lots going on, somewhere that would always surprise. It would have all the things that any other successful district would have.[10] Argent saw the opportunity to become an exemplar of place-making practice within the UK real-estate community.

Planning permission imposed the requirement that residential and community facilities be used to support and regenerate local facilities. It also asked for a place of distinct identity that enhanced the features of historic and conservation importance and, in 2005, gave explicit provision for health and education facilities, green energy and more green open space. In 2008, the three development parties – Argent, London and Continental Railways, and DHL – formed a joint partnership, Kings Cross Central Ltd Partnership, the single landowner at Kings Cross.

Taking time to develop the vision in conjunction with local stakeholders paid off – the facilities now include two major public buildings, and the London Borough of Camden council offices, which also include open access to the library, café, gym, fitness centre and indoor swimming pool, and the Central St Martins College, part of the University of the Arts, London. Students are already on site in the Urban Nest student housing, and the Rubicon social housing is occupied: part of the 1,946 housing units to be provided.

A public realm of open space in the form of ten public squares, twenty acres of public space, and access to the canal is ongoing, and cafés, restaurants and retail units are beginning to appear along with some of the twenty new streets. Excellent public transport including connection to Eurostar ensures it is easy to reach. Camley Street urban park and Kings Place concert venue are within a five-minute walk.

Commercial offices in separate buildings have been let out as head-quarters buildings and, as office buildings come on stream, tenants will be selected to reflect London and all its diversity.

To create a new sense of 'place' for residents and visitors alike, the importance of public spaces, connections, ways through and places to linger was a catalyst for the development of the whole. Occupying 40 per cent of the site, each space is different, with an emphasis on being fun and unpredictable. Temporary public spaces are constructed, which are designed to intrigue while sites are awaiting development. Recognising the importance of this strategy was a tremendously successful move in encouraging people to visit more than once, especially in the early days. Kings Boulevard, the main north–south route, is deliberately not laid straight to give a sense of surprise and playfulness. Landscapes change seasonally, contributing to the vitality of the area. Water is a feature. Undulating water fountains by day change into colourful-light water sculptures by night. There are resting places along the canal, and amphitheatre steps down to the canal towpath. Walking and cycling are the only transportation methods used through the site, as cars and vans are permitted for deliveries only.

Retailing will be diverse. Necessarily, the first to open was the Grain Store, a café–restaurant conversion to accompany the first converted offices and the main public square. Street-food traders have been trialled with some success.

Housing is another major component, spread over thirteen different residential units and of great interest to investors and residents. One hundred and twenty seven 'affordable' homes (flats) have been designed by award-winning housing architects and built in a group of varying heights around three cores to create a sense of community on each floor. A high proportion of these have dual aspect, all have bat- and bird-boxes and access to their own, managed, shared, roof garden.

Sustainability and reduced energy use is evident in all aspects of the Kings Cross regeneration. Energy efficient initiatives have been trialled, heritage buildings have been reused, green transportation policies have been implemented, and the Building Research Environmental Energy Assessment Measurement of 'excellent' and accreditation have been awarded to the three completed office buildings.

The site has the largest combined heat and power plant in the country, supplying green energy across the site. Each building is connected to this central supply, dispensing with the need for individual boilers and associated plant, and resulting in a 5 per cent reduction in energy bills. High-efficiency engines are to be installed in the future, allowing an offset of 80 per cent of the power demand. Solar panels, ground-source heat pumps and solar thermal systems bring about a 50 per cent reduction in carbon emissions compared with average levels in surrounding boroughs in 2005.

Most buildings have green or brown roofs, offering natural cooling – a wonderful resource – and a home for flora and fauna. Green walls, nine hundred bicycle parking spaces and the diversion of 81 per cent of waste from landfill (in 2013) are exemplary statistics. Community involvement is active in the Global Generation skip garden, constructed mainly from building-site waste materials with planting in skips and portable containers. The garden educates children and adults in sustainable buildings and lifestyles, grows food and flowers, keeps hens and is also an example of the growing interaction between the local community and the development. The skip garden teaches all ages how to grow, make, market and sell food, engaging many skills including social enterprise.

One of the delights available to the public in 2015 was the London Pond Club open-air swimming pond, its water cleaned through plant filtration without chemicals. Argent participates enthusiastically in the annual London Open House 'green sky thinking' and other green information-sharing initiatives. Publicity and openness have helped build trust and social capital on this vast site, supported by an active events programme with food festivals, film screenings and a year-round calendar of public events partly paid for by service charges.

Maintaining longevity for the development was secured by long-lease arrangements with the London Borough of Camden, Google and BNP Paribas on the basis that they won't trade out. Argent is similarly committed to the long term, when financially there could have been a temptation to see the site as a package of plots to be sold off. Argent have had to be flexible over their business plan, financial strategy and master plan to keep meeting their stated criteria.

The London Plan 2011

The development of London including the identification and inclusion of brownfield sites has been addressed in the Mayor of London's London Plan 2011,[11] which sets out strategies for managing London over the next ten years. It shows London continuing its established population growth and sets out a provisional target with an annual average of 42,000 additional homes across London to be reviewed by

2019/2020, setting annual targets for each borough to achieve the overall amount.

In the Housing Supplementary Planning Guidance document 2012[12] – the implementation framework to the Mayor of London's 2011 plan, strategies are laid out to provide the increased housing supply. It encourages housing development in 'Opportunity' and 'Intensification' areas, recognises the challenge facing regeneration areas, identifies the particular potential of East London and the designated development corridors, and addresses the needs of the Olympic legacy area. Brownfield sites across London are listed for further exploration with regard to growth and mixed-use development.

The ten areas selected for intensification have significant potential for increases in residential, employment and other uses through development of sites at higher densities with more mixed and intensive use. The thirty-three zones identified as 'opportunity areas' are locations where large-scale development can provide substantial numbers of new employment and housing – typically up to five thousand jobs and / or two thousand five hundred homes – with mixed and intensive land use. Significantly, the Queen Elizabeth Olympic Park is at the fulcrum of two important growth corridors incorporating significant brownfield sites, the west corridor being London – Stanstead – Cambridge – Peterborough and the west corridor being the Thames Gateway.

The Future – the Changing Nature of Work

Along with housing, the developments above have insisted on studies showing local employment that will be generated as a result of those developments. London's comprehensive transport network enables people to reach their employment.

However, an increasing number of people are working flexible hours and not always in an office. The rising cost of office provision in the capital city offers the opportunity for flexible working. According to *Moneybox Live* on BBC Radio 4, the number of self-employed workers continues to rise and is over five million at present. Cafés, institutions and libraries recognise this and provide free internet access, opening their doors to the new, mobile, work community. These available resources start to become very important whether home is short or long term and the sense of being 'at home' extends to the area where people live and places nearby that feel comfortable in the City.

Changing cityscape usage has highlighted a few housing-related issues:

1. Large developments will continue to be financed by private/ developer partnerships. This can result in less affordable housing than originally anticipated by the local authority. Kings Cross is an example of this. The legal agreement made between the developer and the local authority in order to secure planning permission committed Argent LLP to provide 750 housing units. Eight years later, Argent requested a deed of variation. Both parties acknowledged that many changes had occurred during these eight years: to the economy, politically, a reduction in subsidy from the GLA and changes to affordable housing tenure. Kings Cross Phase 1 had been completed and 289 units delivered. The London Borough of Camden entered into negotiations as the reserved matters of the original agreement provided for the detail to be worked out during the development. Camden too had been affected by the changes over the last eight years such that the council had used public subsidy via the GLA to pay an affordable housing price for Phase 1 to enable the service operator to buy the building from the developer – £37,395,045 in this case, an unsustainable cost. A reduction in numbers of units and alterations to the housing mix were agreed in a deed of variation for Phase 2. See the full Planning Officers report.[13]

2. The increase in London housing prices may put more 'affordable' homes beyond people's reach as wages are not rising at the same rate. The definition of 'affordable homes' is that they are let by local authorities, subject to rent controls and their rent is payable to the council. The rent must be no more than 80 per cent of the local market rate. This calculation is costly to the council as a buoyant 'buy to let' housing market and property purchased by overseas investors who live elsewhere are both pushing up the local market rate for housing in 2015.

3. Future London homes are likely to be high-rise with minimum-sized rooms and living spaces – a whole study could be undertaken on room sizes today compared with previous acceptable standards but that is beyond the scope of this chapter. With tighter living conditions, a clean, sustainable city, the public realm and facilities available outside the home become all the

more important for well-being in terms of working, meeting, studying, recreation, stimulation and health.

4. Joint ventures with commercial developers who have loans to secure and repay will inevitably mean that planners must be trained to carry out the tough negotiations that will be required to ensure social housing objectives are met and are the best deal for residents and the wider public alike.

5. Securing developments for longevity has been demonstrated as incredibly important and requires significant time working with local and neighbouring areas. Considerable time for dialogue and interaction is necessary to bring together ways of improving the existing environment in preference to implementing a purely commercial and much quicker installation. A financial framework to secure the developer on these terms is essential. Successful brownfield sites developed along these lines will have the capacity to impact positively on the surrounding areas as people are drawn to the whole neighbourhood.

6. The whole environment, especially the public spaces, is important, and commitment is needed to bring appropriate new initiatives to public areas.

7. Sustainability has been a strong element to all the schemes – there has to be continued political will and support to maintain this momentum.

Chapter Six

Green Space and Housing

Helen Woolley

Green space is an important part of daily life in the UK, and has the possibility of being most frequently used and appreciated if it is close to home and of a good quality. It can take many different forms and provide a wide range of benefits. This is the focus of this chapter, which will explore something of the relationship between green space and housing from the beginning of the twentieth century until now. It is not a full historic discussion but some aspects of the possible relationship between housing and the green space within which it is set provide context for the current need for housing. Some major opportunities and benefits of housing green spaces are discussed, in particular children's play and food-growing, while housing density which has a close relationship with the provision of green space is also briefly addressed.

Garden Villages to Streets in the Sky: Differences in Provision of Green Space

Cadbury's are famous for the chocolate that they make but what people who enjoy the chocolate, particularly the dark chocolate called Bournville, may not realise is that Bournville is the name of the garden village several miles south of the UK's second biggest city, Birmingham, where the chocolate factory is located. When the factory originated in the centre of Birmingham, George Cadbury became concerned about the speculative house-builders of the time and the poor quality of the living environments that were being provided. George Cadbury had been brought up in the wealthy area of Birmingham called Edgbaston where he had a garden providing him opportunities for contact with nature, and he wanted his workforce to have similar opportunities. This experience, together with his Quaker faith and moral ethics, drove him to seek to find a new location for the chocolate factory away from the industrialised city centre where he could build a factory and provide good-quality housing for his employees.[1]

Bournville was laid out capitalising on the existing brook, the Bourn, retaining a wood and providing a village green, a green triangle, streets with trees and named after them, recreation and sports grounds, allotments and individual gardens. Gardens were of a specified size, 400 to 800 square yards, which was deemed to be appropriate to provide opportunities for growing fruit and vegetables and allowing children to play. Early tenancy agreements required tenants to maintain their gardens in 'good condition and properly cultivated'.[2] Gardening associations allowed for benefits such as bulk-buying of tools and seeds, and indeed seemed to have provided a level of neighbourhood peer pressure which assisted in keeping the gardens well maintained.[3] Cadbury understood that this approach of maximising contact with nature and providing good-quality housing a walkable distance from work would support health, welfare and social benefits.

Some of these benefits were evidenced in George Cadbury's research: girls and boys in Bournville were heavier (a good thing in those days) and two or three inches taller than boys and girls elsewhere in Birmingham; the death rate in Bournville was lower than in Birmingham, and England and Wales; and infant mortality in Bournville was 51 per 1,000 compared to 101 for Birmingham and 97 across England and Wales.[4] The approach of an overall plan with good-quality housing and connected private and public green spaces of different types was also taken by Joseph Rowntree in the development of New Earswick in York, Titus Salt in Saltaire near Bradford, and the Lever Brothers' development of Port Sunlight on Merseyside. Following the success of the garden village of Bournville, the Bournville Village Trust undertook a social study of the living and working conditions in Birmingham to help inform the reconstruction of it and other towns and cities after World War II.[5] The research discussed a range of issues including travel time to work and suggested that it was important for everyone to live reasonably near their work. The importance of gardens for children's play and existence of parks and open spaces as lungs of the city were also emphasised. Interestingly the report includes a lengthy discussion about gardens with the conclusion that, 'Birmingham people really do like their gardens'.[6]

As a child of the late 1950s and early 1960s, my childhood experience of Bournville was set in the context of the trees named after local streets, including the delight of yellow when the laburnum trees were in flower on Laburnum Road, playing Pooh Sticks on the bridge over the Bourn brook, walking to the village green and then through the parks, and throwing sticks up the horse chestnut tree to get the conkers to fall down in the autumn. I certainly had contact with nature. My social experience was enhanced by the infant and junior schools across the road from the green, the village shops and annual events such as singing carols on Christmas Eve around the tree on the green, and preparation for and dancing around the maypole (the largest in the country) on the men's recreation ground, next to the chocolate factory, for the annual Bournville Village Festival. My church community was not in the village, because there was no Baptist church and this was the Christian tradition I was brought up in and continue to follow. However, my experience of growing up in Bournville was definitely one of the drivers to my decision to become a landscape architect with a conviction that other people should have the opportunity to live in good-quality housing set in a variety of connected green spaces, giving multiple opportunities for contact with nature and children's play.

The garden cities movement pioneered by Ebenezer Howard took some of the concepts of garden villages into housing settlements of larger sizes including Letchworth and Welwyn Garden City. Again the inclusion of green spaces was an important consideration. The new towns were the next wave of housing settlements to affirm the importance of green spaces with Telford, Washington and Milton Keynes being some of the most well known. The green spaces in these developments also tended to be connected, providing routes for walking and cycling although, by the time of the development of the later new towns, the car was dominating many of the urban planning decisions and approaches. In the post-war period, some of the reconstruction was influenced by the modernist approach, which resulted in tower blocks and the streets in the sky of Park Hill, Hyde Park and the Kelvin flats in Sheffield. These developments included green space. Usually this was in the form of grass and occasional trees and a fixed equipment playground of some type. Opportunities for real contact with nature and exploration were limited.

The priority given to the extent, diversity and connectivity of green spaces in the garden villages, garden cities and to some extent the new towns resulted in an overall sense of ownership of these green spaces by communities. Another result was the density of these developments, which was low. Many of the post-World War II developments were not only increasingly dominated by cars but also consisted of higher-density housing where the quality of the green spaces and the experience for the communities was of a poorer quality.

Evidence: Affirming the Importance of Green Space in Housing Areas

We have already seen that George Cadbury and the Bournville Village Trust undertook research around issues relating to housing, green space and travel. They were pioneers not only in the housing provision but also in undertaking this research, which is probably little known about. During the last forty or so years, a raft of research has confirmed the importance of green space in housing areas for different reasons. Little of this research has been undertaken in the UK but some key pieces are worth mentioning, partly because some specifically focus on children's play in housing areas. Two of these were large pieces of research undertaken in the 1960s and 1970s, the first on twelve housing estates and the second using fifty thousand observations on fifteen housing estates. Both revealed that children did not only play in the designated playgrounds but also on roads, pavements and car parks, paved areas, public grass and gardens, paved areas, wild areas, planted areas, access walls and fences and the flat rooves of garages.[7] *Children at Play* also revealed that children living on the higher floors of high-rise buildings were less likely to play out than those living on the lower floors.

Similar findings about the spaces in the housing area that children used for play were revealed in more recent research, which identified that some of the locations were used because children could spontaneously meet up with friends. Moving around on foot and bicycle was important and facilitated by the existence of footpaths, and was part of the experience of meeting up with friends. Estates with traffic calming, street closures, walls, driveways and culs-de-sac were the most supportive of children's play.[8] More recent research has reconfirmed the importance of paths in housing areas for the social connections and play opportunities they can support.[9]

Paths are also important for older people, who like to have pleasant and safe neighbourhood open spaces within a comfortable walking distance from home. But it is not just the existence of paths that are important; they need to be easy to walk on, enjoyable and have no obstacle to getting into the open space.[10] One of the key issues identified for older people was the importance of having an open space within ten minutes from their homes. This is not a new finding, with various previous pieces of research revealing the importance of green spaces being close to where people live. In contemporary social housing areas, people may spend most of their time in their homes and neighbourhoods and because of this the quality, design and management of the green open spaces that the housing is set in is of vital importance for people of all ages.

Types of Green Space: Gardens, Housing Green Spaces and Allotments

In understanding that green spaces associated with housing areas provide benefits – such as contact with nature, opportunities for play and walking, social connections and health – it is helpful to consider the different types of green and open spaces that can support these benefits. Elsewhere I have described that urban open spaces can be domestic, neighbourhood and civic, and it is the former two types which are most relevant to housing areas while civic spaces relate more to town and city centres, health, education, transport and city-wide recreation facilities.[11] The private domestic open spaces of gardens have already been discussed in the discourse about village and garden cities. Some mention has also been made of the open spaces within which housing is set, in that tower blocks took the modernist approach with the result that large areas of grass were provided with the intention that they would be communal space but, in reality, instead of being *everybody's* space they became *nobody's* space. This has left large areas of land in the UK's major cities within the remit of councils or social housing providers with green spaces that have become unused and often looking neglected. Generally these housing providers prioritise the built form and tend to ignore the community green spaces. However, in recent years some providers have worked to make forgotten green spaces used by communities while improving the quality of the open spaces.

One such project, funded by the BIG Lottery Reaching Communities programme in Sheffield, was called Living with Nature. One housing officer who heard me speak at an event contacted me about her concerns about the quality of the outdoor play spaces she was responsible for maintaining. Over a period of seven years, we worked in partnership on workshops, seminars, student projects and the development of a play strategy, the latter with the support of CABE Space (for whom I was an enabler). This culminated in a three-year project working with communities in twenty-four social housing areas across the city. The aim was to improve the quality of some of the housing green spaces for the dual benefits of children's play and biodiversity. In reality, and unexpectedly, the project also supported communities to re-engage with these forgotten green spaces and, two years on from the end of the project, several of the communities organise their own activities and fund-raising events for money to continue the improvement of the physical environment. One community has just organised the fifth year of annual activities including a dog show and a sports day, while another had an event on site with four hundred people – so popular that people came from outside the immediate community to enjoy themselves. Some of the community groups work with others providing support in organisation and, in one instance, donating fruit trees to a community group on the other side of the city. It is a credit to the key staff of the project that there is an ongoing legacy: this project is not only about the improved play opportunities and biodiversity but also about the sense of community cohesion it has generated and which is continuing to drive many of the twenty-four projects forward.

Food-Growing Spaces

A small component of Living with Nature has been food-growing in the form of community growing areas and a 'crumble garden' on one site. Growing food, which was a core of the green and healthy approach of the garden villages, has a tradition of being undertaken not only in gardens but also in the neighbourhood green spaces of allotments since Anglo-Saxon times. In Birmingham, allotments have been part of the urban framework since before 1731, with the peak in numbers of these 'guinea gardens' being between 1820 and 1830.[12] For many people who moved from the country to the city, allotments provided an ongoing connection with the countryside and an opportunity to supplement their low wages with freshly grown fruit and vegetables. Initially these gardens were privately owned but the Allotments Acts of 1887 and 1890 resulted in local authorities also providing allotments and they continue to be the main providers. The number of allotments in the UK rose from half a million in 1913 to one and a half million by 1918 at the end of World War I. Between the wars, some of the allotments were retained while others were used for housing development, and the 1925 Allotments Act required allotments to be included in town plans.

World War II brought about a need for home-grown food, and the Dig for Victory campaign also led to an increase in the number of allotments. Figures available for Birmingham, again as an example of a city, show that the city council controlled 11,716 plots at the beginning of the war, increasing to 20,417 plots in 1944.[13] Once again, after the war, many of the plots were used for much-needed housing. By 1965, one fifth of all allotment land in the UK lay vacant and a government allotments advisory committee identified that some of the unpopularity of allotments was a result of issues including security of tenure and compensation for disturbance. The resultant Thorpe Report (1969) suggested a range of legislative, administrative, design and planning changes. It also uncovered that most users were using their allotments for recreational purposes rather than the economic purpose of food growing. One result was the creation of 'leisure gardens', where allotment sites were redesigned to include toilets, piped water, storage, car parking and secure fencing or gates.

In recent years, there has been a resurgence in the popularity of allotments as part of a move by some towards sustainability and self-sufficiency. Currently there are three hundred thousand allotment plots with a waiting list of ninety thousand.[14] The provision of land for allotments could be taken forward as a policy by national and local government with the increasing concerns that exist currently around food security.

Gardens, housing green spaces and allotments are not the only green spaces in our towns and cities that can support food-growing. One internationally well-known project is that of Incredible Edible in Todmorden in West Yorkshire.[15] Todmorden hosted the most productive cotton mill in the country and was a rich market town but, as the production of cotton and clothing changed internationally, the town lost employment opportunities and its income declined. As a response to this, some members of the community decided to start growing food with the aim of increasing the amount of food grown and eaten locally, and the project started in 2008. Fruit and vegetables are grown on all sorts of small, often otherwise unused spaces. These include a green route, incorporating different sites which have been planted, Pollination Street, a soap garden and a recently designed apothecary garden next to the contemporary health centre, all of which include concise educational information about individual plants, bees and other insects. Many small spaces have been planted up with fruit trees and shrubs and edible flowering plants, and these spaces include a small area next to the canal bridge where bottles and cans used to be left, the garden areas in front of the police station, a larger area by the indoor market, and many small incidental spaces in locations adjacent to the canal, car parks, roads and within gardens. Anyone can join in the project and help with planting, and anyone can pick the fruit.

Containing Cities: Providing for Housing Needs and Green Space

So within our towns and cities there is a wide range of different open spaces that support people and biodiversity in and around housing, and we have considered some contemporary examples of where people are seeking to improve the quality of those existing green spaces while working with communities and increasing community capacity. But there is what seems to be an ever-repeating need for new housing. The current increasing pressure for house-building, which for many reasons is a repeated social need and political driver, raises many questions as to where such new housing should be provided and the form that it might take. Surely it would be ideal if all new housing could be provided in the form of low-density housing within a network of different green spaces as epitomised in the garden villages or garden cities. But this would result in much of our agricultural land being built upon to accommodate the increasing population.

The main tool in place to restrict the urbanisation of agricultural land is the green belt, which was a planning tool introduced through the 1947 Town and Country Planning Act. This is what its name suggests: a belt of green land around a city which has a legal remit within which building should not take place, acting as a buffer between the city and the country. Currently 1.6 million hectares of land, 13 per cent of the land area, in England are designated as green belt. From time to time there are threats to the future of the green belt and this must surely be the case now. If the green belt is to be retained and the countryside, where food growing and production is a priority, is to be retained for this purpose, if not increased because of the increasing population, how can the current increased demand for housing be accommodated?

One policy directive of the Labour government of 1997 to 2010 was that 60 per cent of new housing should be built on previously developed land in towns and cities, commonly called brownfield sites; this still left a need for 40 per cent to be built elsewhere, presumably in the countryside. There is no such directive under the current Conservative government and indeed they have changed the planning system to be in favour of sustainable development, without an adequate definition of 'sustainable', while loosening planning controls in the National Planning Policy Framework. One of the acknowledged aims of these changes is economic: to encourage house-building as a driver to the economy. The previous drive for reusing brownfield land was seen by some as good stewardship of urban land and generally it was, although even then there were many situations where larger Victorian and Edwardian homes were converted to flats with new building taking place in the gardens, resulting in a loss of urban green space.

If use of brownfield sites cannot accommodate all the required housing and there is a desire to retain the green belt and protect the countryside, then the only other way to provide an increase in housing is to go upwards, creating multi-storey blocks of flats. In doing this, the provision of a variety of good-quality green spaces becomes problematic, raising questions such as:

- Is there enough physical space to provide a network of green spaces?

- Will developers provide them or will they perceive them as a waste of an economically viable development opportunity?

- Will planners (be able to) insist on the provision of green spaces?

- Will they be too shady or windy to use because of the number of high-rise buildings in the vicinity?

- Would people use such green spaces, considering the evidence that children will not play in a green space if they live too far up a block of flats?

I have visited some of the Chinese mega-cities and been appalled to see that children live in apartment blocks thirty or more storeys high. I would certainly not want British children to live in such accommodation.

So there are some serious questions which need to be debated at national, local and community levels. Green space in our towns and cities is important for social, health, environmental and economic reasons,[16] and we have seen that there are some very specific benefits of green spaces within close proximity of where people live, including children's play, food-growing, walking and biodiversity. As the country seeks how to accommodate its housing needs in the future, I hope and pray that the importance of such green spaces will not be lost but will be at the forefront of the discussion and decision-making at all levels of governance and with all types of housing providers.

Chapter Seven

Lessons on Rural Housing from Scotland

Raymond Young

Scotland is a land of mountains, glens, sea – and tenements! The countryside is what attracts the tourists; the tenements have been the subject of countless housing studies. They give Scotland's towns and cities a distinct urban quality. And the issues surrounding urban housing have a tendency to overshadow the challenges of rural housing. In 1988 a seminal report published by a now long-gone organisation – Rural Forum – was called *Scotland's Rural Housing: A Forgotten Problem.*[1] And while there has been much progress in the last twenty-five or so years, some of the key issues highlighted by that report remain about housing in the countryside.

But first a reminder that Scottish housing has its own distinct history and tradition. The 1707 Act of Union did not bring uniformity to housing within Great Britain. The Scottish legal system and land tenure continued to develop in their own ways, just as the established church had a different structure and approach from those in England and Wales. Housing legislation may have been passed by MPs in Westminster, but for Scotland its administration was carried out in Edinburgh. And even when GB legislation was promoted, for example, the 1974 Housing Act that brought the promotion, registration and funding of housing associations (including Housing Association Grant, HAG), its implementation was tailored to the local situation. Scotland's first First Minister, Donald Dewar, may have coined the phrase 'Scottish solutions for Scottish problems', but it simply reinforced the approach over the centuries.

The fundamental impact of devolution since 1999 on Scottish housing is that ministers responsible for housing are accountable to Holyrood rather than Westminster. They are more accessible, and have been able to focus more on 'Scottish solutions'. But it also means a further division between housing policy and people support between the two parliaments – development (Holyrood) and housing benefit

(Westminster). The potential of a clash between the two turned into reality over welfare and in particular the so-called 'bedroom tax', where the Scottish Parliament has allocated resources to mitigate the impact on individual families. Further devolution will give the Scottish Parliament more power over welfare issues, but not completely.

Rural Scotland

For most of the twentieth century, Scotland's housing policies focused on urban Scotland. During the last two centuries, Scotland has been one of the fastest urbanising nations in the world. Its place at the heart of the Industrial Revolution meant that the demand for (cheap) labour in its burgeoning cities made it attractive for immigrants. The Industrial Revolution, accompanied by transport infrastructure changes, also applied to what had been an agriculture-based nation. It applied to the supporting industries as well – smaller local quarries, metal-working and supply chains. Agricultural changes in farming led to depopulation across the country. In some places, whole communities were moved to make way for new agricultural practices and while the Highland Clearances have a particular resonance and notoriety for most of us (and may have seen some of the worst examples of inhumanity in these islands), the depopulation applied right across the countryside.

The population that moved into towns and cities were housed in cheaply built, poor-quality housing, and these properties came to dominate housing policy in the twentieth century. Privately owned slums were replaced by public-sector housing to the point where nearly 70 per cent of Scots had a public-sector landlord. In the 1970s, there began a reversal of area clearance in favour of rehabilitation – much of which has been carried out by community-based housing associations. In the last twenty years of the twentieth century and the early years of this one, the dominant issue has been the break-up of council estates, either through 'right to buy' or through large-scale transfers.

Meanwhile, as its population declined, rural Scotland became romantic Scotland. Boswell started it, and people like Sir Walter Scott exploited it and Queen Victoria blessed it. The romance remains, promoted mainly by people who live in cities. We see rural Scotland through the visitor gaze, without really trying to understand what life must be like now for those who want to make their living from the sea, the land or from a large number of non-agricultural activities and without whom we would not be able to enjoy one of the most beautiful and best bits on God's earth. We treat rural Scotland like a vast theme park, a pleasure dome, full of exotica from which we retreat back to our townie life. And we like it that way. We get up in arms when someone wants to develop and change that countryside. We want rural Scotland to stay the way we imagine it. We often do not recognise the variety of employment and opportunities that there are outside our urban existence.

The Scottish Government has developed an urban / rural classification that defines settlements with a population of three thousand or fewer to be rural.[2] It also classifies areas as remote, based on drive time. Accessible areas are those that are within a thirty-minute drive from the centre of a settlement with a population of ten thousand or more, while remote areas have a drive-time that is greater than thirty minutes. Eighteen per cent of Scots (nearly 1 million) live in rural Scotland (6 per cent remote, 12 per cent accessible), in 94 per cent of the land mass (69 per cent remote). There are ninety-four inhabited islands.[3] And the population is growing – particularly in accessible areas where growth is three times the national average. The challenge of providing housing is compounded by the land ownership, where more than half the total land is owned by five hundred people in what Jim Hunter, author, academic and reformer, has described as 'the most concentrated pattern of land ownership in the developed world'.[4]

Rural Scotland is not just a visitors' paradise. Tourism may now be its biggest industry, but agriculture, aquaculture and arboriculture still have a bright future, along with energy supply and other larger-scale industries, while SMEs, the arts and education are thriving. And all of these need support services from posties to procurator fiscals, from nurses to neurosurgeons, from mechanics to masons. And all this means that people need somewhere to live. Unlike many other developed countries, Scotland is enjoying an increase in population in its rural communities – including in some of the most remote areas. The lifestyle may be what many people want; and different people seek different lifestyles. For many it is an escape from the hustle and bustle of the big cities – they seek quiet and want to live the dream they have hankered after for years. For some it is a combination of living in the countryside while commuting to a city job. For others it is an opportunity to bring up a family in an area where commuting is not required, in what is perceived as a crime-free environment and where the community is made up of people who look out for one another. For others still it is an opportunity to return to their family roots, or to develop land- or sea-based employment. Rural Scotland means many things to many people. And rural Scotland is not homogeneous. For such a small country, the variety is enormous. The Highlands and Islands are considerably different from the north east, which is different from the south west and it is different from its neighbour in the Scottish Borders. Culture, language, dialect, agriculture, weather and population density are varied across the country.

Rural development in Scotland is carefully managed. The views may be spectacular, but you can't live in a view. If you have plenty of money you will have little difficulty in purchasing a house or buying land and building one. Indeed you may well outbid someone on modest or low income. Gentrification is becoming a major issue in rural Scotland. Affordable housing to rent or buy remains in short supply. And thus – particularly if you are young – you may find yourself having to stay with relatives, or sleep on a friend's floor or in a caravan. Or you may have to abandon your plan to work and live in the countryside. In areas where tourism is the main industry, you may be able to rent a house for the winter, but have to find somewhere else to live during 'the season'. And those on 'modest income' can include the teacher, the nurse, the fisherman, the plumber, the joiner, the chef and the hotel receptionist, all of which are key jobs to ensure the economic and social future of rural Scotland.

In addition, the infrastructure in many places is poor. Development costs are high. There are few builders and the supply chain is difficult. Islands and some isolated communities depend on boats and planes. Ferries may be busy in the summer, but in the winter they are lifeline services supported by the government. Much of the road is single-track. And to get some sense of the scale of challenge, the coastline of one region of south-west Scotland – Argyll, which includes Mull and Iona – is longer than the coastline of France.

So how has Scotland responded to the challenge of providing affordable homes? Over the last one hundred years, there have been specific policies and programmes for housing in its rural areas. The oldest is now called the Croft Grant House Scheme. Crofting is an agricultural way of life and a unique tenure in the west coast and islands in which the crofter has security of tenure on land that he or she does not own. That tenure requires the crofter to provide their own house and the lack of land ownership precludes access to conventional forms of finance. The scheme, over the years, provided grants and loans, managed by the Department of Agriculture and Fisheries. This also included an architectural service with standard house plans and government-owned agricultural depots provided building materials.

In 1989, a national housing agency was established – Scottish Homes. Its first strategic policy development was a rural housing policy in 1990, for which I was lead officer. Based on research, on market analysis and the experience of practitioners – particularly housing associations – it set out a wide menu of programmes designed to support the provision of home ownership and rented accommodation, recognising the challenges and variety across rural Scotland. Primarily it was about creating affordable housing. Since then, government support for housing has come direct from the government itself. Over the years, housing policy has moved from simply being about bricks and mortar, supply and condition. It has become part of the government's procurement policy and integrated into its regeneration agenda. There is no separate rural housing section within the government's housing strategy.

Access to affordable housing comes in three ways – through low-cost home ownership, by renting from the private sector, or by renting from a social-housing landlord. All three suffer from pressure – where demand outstrips supply.

In the private sector, there is very little speculative housebuilding except in accessible areas, and these tend to be 'up market'. Over the last thirty years, there have been numerous attempts by governments to stimulate home ownership, which would be the preferred choice of most people. Seventy-five per cent of rural homes are owner-occupied. A number of low-cost home-ownership (LCHO) initiatives have been developed; some have been very short-term and on the whole have been similar to those for urban areas. One particular programme was designed specifically with rural areas in mind. Scottish Homes LCHO powers enabled the creation of a grant to individuals which was modelled on the crofter grants scheme. The argument was that the second and third sons and daughters of the croft could get a piece of ground from their crofter parent or senior sibling (whoever was the crofter), but could not get any assistance with building costs. So a rural home-ownership grant (RHOG) was created. These grants for individuals were not limited to crofting areas. They also encouraged self-build, including some places with serviced plots. RHOGs turned out to be popular in some parts of Scotland – particularly the Highlands and Islands – but elsewhere it was regarded as a bureaucratic nightmare. And there was always the problem of finding a plot. The difficulty of land acquisition is a thread running through attempts to improve affordable housing.

With 11 per cent of the rural housing stock, the private-rental sector is provided mainly by landowners (interestingly the proportion of private renting is greater in the cities). There has been Scottish Government encouragement to landowners to build, and some used a one-off £5 million 'Rural Homes for Rent' grant scheme, launched in 2008. This was also targeted at community groups, with very mixed results – the timescale was short and few community groups were sufficiently organised to be able to take advantage of it. It worked where the land was already in the ownership of the applicant!

In the social housing sector, local authorities are now able to build again after a period when new 'council housing' was disapproved of. The major player providing new lettings over the last twenty-five years has been the voluntary housing association. This comes in three varieties: locally based, covering perhaps a few settlements within a recognisable rural area; regional, with its head office in a rural town but covering a wider area; and national, mainly providing housing for specific groups of people, such as the elderly. Some of them have grown slowly over the years; others have appeared very quickly but with a housing stock that goes back years, having taken over public-sector housing. All have a part to play.[5]

If there is a distinctive feature to housing associations in Scotland, it is the large number of community-based associations. They were conceived for tenement rehabilitation in the 1970s at a time when the committees of associations were largely self-selective.[6] Membership was open to anyone in the area of operation, particularly tenants, and they served a small geographical area. When translated into rural Scotland, they had to operate in a slightly larger area, but on the same principles as their urban counterparts. They tend to be based in a settlement that is the service centre for an area, such as the local market town. Their rented housing stock will be around 1,500, but many also provide home-ownership options, including shared ownership. In the 1990 policy, we called them 'local housing agencies', delivering a range of services that were housing-related. Housing may have been their *raison d'être* but they recognise that, as local anchor organisations, they play a major role in stimulating local construction, in providing energy advice to everyone in the area, and managing the care and repair programmes that keep elderly and disabled people in their own homes for as long as possible. They are key partners with health boards and economic development agencies.

But housing associations are faced with huge challenges. The Thatcher Government's two main housing policies – right to buy (RTB) and stock transfers – have had major impact on the movement. Both were continued under devolution, although RTB was abolished from August 2016. However, in 2001, the Scottish Parliament introduced 'pressured area' status, allowing local authorities to apply from exemption from RTB for five years, which is particularly helpful in affordable rural areas. The transfer of public-sector houses has swelled both the numbers of associations (or registered social landlords [RSLs] as we must now call them) and the size of many existing ones. Although the Glasgow stock transfer to Glasgow Housing Association is the best known, four rural authorities have, with tenants' support, transferred all of their houses to RSLs. The financial challenges that now face RSLs are huge, requiring different skills in both staff and committee members. However, most rural associations have managed to retain their community roots and, although mergers and takeovers have taken place, these tend to be at regional rather than national or GB-wide level. Most associations remain relatively small and locally grounded. But development is constrained by a lack of finance, and many have had to reduce their development capacity. And if they could develop, land once again features as a major challenge.

Scottish Land Reform and Community

'Land' is one of two words that have dominated rural housing discussions in Scotland over the last twenty years. The other is 'community'. They are interlinked.

Land reform has been a key concern of the Scottish Parliament. In the run-up to Holyrood's inception, the Labour Government established a community land unit and fund within Highlands and Islands Enterprise (HIE) to support a growing interest in rural communities in becoming their own landowners. The pattern was set in 1993 when the community of Assynt purchased the North Lochinver estate, in northwest Scotland.[7]

HIE is one of two economic agencies in Scotland; the other is Scottish Enterprise (SE). HIE has social as well as economic responsibilities (unlike SE, which tends to be about large-scale economic initiatives and has virtually no track record in rural issues), and has played a key role in turning round the fortunes of the Highlands and Islands by sensitive local economic development. It works closely with housing agencies because the two go hand in hand.

By 2003, the Scottish Parliament passed the Land Reform (Scotland) Act, which established what has become known as the 'community right to buy', in which communities with a population of fewer than ten thousand can apply to register an interest in the land and to buy that land when it comes up for sale. Legislation now before the Parliament develops the earlier Act by, among other purposes, giving tenant farmers greater security and communities greater powers to acquire land they need for economic and social development.[8] Whether this will solve the land issue remains to be seen. The Scottish Parliamentary Rural Affairs and Environment Committee,[9] with further support by the OECD,[10] has called for greater use of compulsory purchase powers (CPOs). If housing is needed for economic development, should it to be treated as infrastructure – like roads, for which CPOs are the norm?

Some of the key players in the Highlands and Islands – notably Di Alexander, who had worked for Shelter in its Empty Homes Initiative when setting up Lochaber Housing Association – have developed more initiatives to improve land supply. First, a group of associations, along with Highland Council, set up the Highlands Small Communities Housing Trust (HSCHT) as a council-wide land-banking facility. A start-up grant from the government enabled a revolving fund; sites were acquired, then sold either to individuals with RHOG support or to housing associations. A further development was the Highland Housing Alliance, a development company owned by five associations, HSCHT and the council, to help build more homes of all tenures for people in the highlands. In the south west a similar trust – Dumfries and Galloway Housing Trust (D&GHT) – grew out of a rural housing initiative by Shelter.

The next challenge was that of ensuring that the houses remained affordable in perpetuity. The challenge included second homes or locals being outbid in the market (mainly but not exclusively by downsizing retirees who are moving from the south – both Scotland and elsewhere). Enter 'Rural Housing Burdens' (RHB)[11] following further Scottish parliamentary legislation (and another Di Alexander initiative). Under the mechanism, land is acquired at a discounted rate, and the discount is passed on for the benefit of the local community. To operate the system, the housing association or the Community Land Trust (CLT) has first to be designated as a 'rural housing body' by the government. Then the designated body acquires a piece of land at a discounted rate from a landowner and builds houses on the land. When the houses are sold, an RHB is inserted into the title deeds, giving the designated body the right to repurchase the property whenever it is made available for sale. In this way the discount is locked in forever, and the houses remain within the local affordable market rather than being 'lost' to the open market.

The inclusion of CLTs in the RHB mechanism reflected the important role that the development trust movement is playing in the provision of affordable housing in rural areas of Scotland. Communities that had exercised their 'community right to buy' suddenly became owners of estate houses. They could obtain grants to upgrade them, but funding for new rented homes was not available to begin with. So housing associations developed a partnership to build new houses with these new landowners – as in the case of the island of Gigha. But other ways have been found to help these communities. The 'Rural Homes for Rent' scheme was one. On Mull, the Ulva School Community Association is building two houses with funding from the Community Land Trust, Argyll and Bute Council (using the additional council tax fund from second homes) and local fundraising. They are supported by Mull and Iona Community Trust, who are employing a housing manager. On Iona itself, the local housing partnership fought for ten years to buy part of the church's glebe, and is working with West Highland Housing Association to build five homes to rent. Community-driven projects like these will become a major feature in the future with the reduction in grant for housing associations. Many housing associations are facing the future with optimism, energy and ingenuity but, above all, remaining true to their community roots. And the way ahead may be similar to the English Community Land Trusts, where the local community draws on the experience and skills of the local housing association or development trust.

The Iona and Mull groups were two of the many such groups helped by Rural Housing Scotland, (RHS), HSCHT, Shelter and D&GHT. RHS, through its rural housing enabler programme, helps the local community to analyse local housing needs and provides guidance and support on potential housing solutions. Its board (and its annual conference) brings together players from all sectors – including community buy-out groups, housing associations, landowners, academics, and individuals from other agencies. The current chair is the Director of Scottish Churches Housing Action, which is itself working with churches to create affordable housing from redundant buildings and excess land. Consideration is currently being given to a closer working partnership between RHS, HSCHT and D&GHT within a community housing alliance.

Although there is no longer a separate rural housing policy, the range of initiatives coming from Westminster and Holyrood on one hand and local practitioners on the other shows a commitment to meeting the need for affordable housing in Scotland. There are many challenges to overcome. For example, while the quality of rural housing has improved over the years, it still lags behind the Scottish average. Rural Scotland has some of the highest levels of fuel poverty in the UK, with some of the highest fuel costs, particularly since so many homes are 'off gas'.[12] The Scottish Government has recently set up the Scottish Rural Fuel Poverty Task Force to develop practical solutions.

Future development of affordable housing depends on a whole set of factors. Land, finance and delivery organisations and mechanisms are only some of the challenges. There continue to be concerns about a traditional presumption against affordable housing in smaller communities, be it from NIMBYs, or from those who say that only urban communities are sustainable. Scottish planning policy since 2010[13] has encouraged appropriate development, including small-scale development that supports sustainable economic growth. The planning advice note on affordable housing encourages local authorities to be 'sensitive to different levels of need in different parts of the local authority area, particularly in rural areas'. At least this national framework recognises the need for a different approach in rural areas. Such an approach, one that accepts the need for 'rural proofing', is to be welcomed. And at its heart is the need to empower rural communities to be in charge of their own destiny. Perhaps a lesson for the rest of the UK as well?

Chapter Eight

For Richer and Richer...

Paul Lusk

Generation Rent

Fifty years ago, Britain had 16.5 million homes and a population of 51.3 million – one home for every 3.1 people. The average house price was about three times the annual wage of a male industrial worker. So reader, if you are in your twenties, your grandfather (though not your grandmother) could very likely afford the mortgage on a house if in regular work. By the 1990s, there was one home for every 2.5 people, and prices – at about four times average annual wage – still left purchase within the reach of your working parents, especially with a second salary taken into account. Now there are nearly 28 million homes for a population of 64 million – one home for every 2.3 people – but the average price,[1] at around seven times average annual salary, puts house purchase beyond the reach of most employees. Welcome to Generation Rent.

The conventional wisdom is that there are too few homes for the demand, and prices reflect this shortfall, so the only response is to build more homes. This leaves a question as to why, in real terms after allowing for general inflation, house prices have more than trebled in thirty years while the growth in the housing stock has more than kept up with that of population.[2] So is there really a housing 'shortage'? Is that an adequate explanation of house-price movements? If not, what else is going on in our housing markets?

My answer will consider the three ways we occupy homes – as owners, as social tenants, and as private tenants – against the background of 'welfare state' housing as it developed in the second half of the last century. I will show that the 'housing crisis' is really about distribution, though there may still be a case for developing housing unit numbers. The distribution crisis arises mostly from welfare housing policies and their uneven effect. Public discussion of housing is shot through with propaganda, wilful ignorance and the subordination of evidence to political myth. Truth can free us from myth, but only if we can first acknowledge the stake which most of us (including this writer and the majority of voters) have in its construction. This may be painful but we owe Generation Rent an explanation of the mess we are leaving them to live with.

Please Please Me: The Rise and Fall of Owner-Occupation

Let's start with those grandparents and parents – the people who grew up with the National Health Service and gave birth to more of their number into the 1970s. Having been a teenager when the Beatles topped the hit parade, I think of us as the Please Please Me generation – the one that learnt to take for granted free healthcare, free education and free love. Mostly we got homes for free. *Free*? Yes – if you consider that growth in house prices more than covered the cost of borrowing. An average buyer in 1969 saw the cash value of their home grow by over 10 per cent a year for the life of a twenty-five-year mortgage, when interest rates were generally at or below this figure. Then from 1994 to 2007, house values continued the same rate of growth but now interest rates were at or below 6 per cent. Over the forty years up to 2007, the consumer mindset became fixed as 'Borrow as much on mortgage as we can; it will more than pay for itself'. And then with relaxed financial controls, a corresponding mindset entered the banks: 'Lend as much on mortgage as we can; our balance sheets can only get fatter.' The crash of 2008 was the result, largely, of the house-price Ponzi scheme that printed money for the Please Please Me generation.

To understand this, we need to look back to the creation of the post-war welfare state and in particular to the thought of T.H. Marshall. In *Citizenship and Social Class*,[3] Marshall said that in a modern democracy, three goods are to be provided to all to a basic standard. These are health, education and housing. Citizens have a 'social right' to these. Health, education and housing can all be provided through the market, but giving people money to buy them does not promote equality – giving poorer people money might help the poor but it squeezes out those in the middle who cannot compete with the self-funded rich and the state-aided poor. The answer, according to Marshall, is state supply to a roughly equal standard for all. He expected that, in time, council housing would be like education and the health service – provided by the state and available to everyone on more or less equal terms.

By the mid-1970s, one UK household in three was a tenant of the state, but the major form of tenure became owner-occupation. Sustained growth in house prices dates from 1959, when the House

Purchase and Housing Act empowered government to fund building societies to increase lending for older and cheaper homes. Soon after, Schedule A income tax for owner-occupiers – which taxed the 'imputed rent' flowing from land ownership – was abolished. Meanwhile tax relief on mortgage interest – which counted as a cost for Schedule A purposes – was kept. So now both public finance and subsidy promoted borrowing for home ownership. House prices grew and profits on sales by residents were exempt from tax.

In 2015, nearly half of owner-occupiers no longer have mortgages – they are 'debt-free'. Most households headed by a pensioner are in this category. Among homeowners with mortgages, the average mortgage debt is £83,000, and their household income, at £43,000, is £10,000 above the national average. Most of these spend under a third of their income on servicing their debt, and could comfortably deal with a rise in interest rates.[4] So the majority of the population pays either nothing, or a comfortably affordable sum, for their housing. This majority represents older people and the more affluent.

Those wishing to enter home ownership face restrictions imposed on lenders by the Bank of England. They (mostly) cannot borrow more than 4.5 times the household income, and a 'stress test' examines their ability to cope with a rise in interest rates by three percentage points within five years.[5] With starter rates for mortgages now at around 2.5 per cent, this means allowing for rates to more than double in five years. The stated aim of these restrictions is to limit (though not prevent) the expected rise in house prices.[6] The effect is that the cost of capital to new homeowners is artificially calculated to equal the rate of return (up to 6 per cent) generally offered to private investors in the rental market – in other words, to prevent new buyers from competing on price with private investors who can borrow cheaply and interest-only on a 75 per cent loan-to-value ratio.

As the Housing Minister told a parliamentary enquiry in September 2015: 'Government is determined to create a bigger, better private rented sector.' The main means to achieve this aim is to limit the flow of new homeowners, so that the medium for allocating stock to new (mainly younger) households is private investment and rental rather than the earlier tradition of mortgage-funded home ownership.

The Fall and Rise of Private Renting

The post-war vision of housing for all was fulfilled – but not by the single form of state tenure that Marshall had expected. Under Thatcher,

Major and Blair, council housing gradually declined – giving way first to the 'right to buy', then to stock transfer as governments grew housing associations as the preferred provider of what became known as 'social housing'. Owner-occupation peaked at 69 per cent of the stock in 2003. By 2010 the share of housing associations in the stock was overtaking that of council housing. But the big story became the return of private renting. In the five years to 2013, as the UK housing stock grew by 648,000, the number of owner-occupiers dropped by 380,000 and the number of privately rented homes rose by 930,000. Privately rented homes now amount to about one home in five. If these trends continue, private renting will overtake owner-occupation before 2040. And government policy is 'determined' that these trends should continue.

Housing: How Do We Occupy It?
Most people in Britain expect to live in a durably constructed enclosure fixed to land. These dwellings can easily last for a century or more. The predominant type of dwelling in the UK is a three-bedroomed house, and one of these might once have been occupied by a single family with two or three generations under one roof, but now with little adaptation it can provide for several unrelated, single income-earners. Most of us see this kind of turnover, in all directions, happening around us.

In theory, the better the housing market, the more efficiently the people looking for homes will fit into the available stock. This implies that there must be a way of drawing some people out of homes when their occupation of that property is no longer an efficient use of space. In a pure, free rental market, all this is done by price expressed as the rent charged – the rent purchases a right to occupy space for a period of time. Owners need to be able to refix the rent regularly, and tenants can only occupy the property for a fixed term. These are the conditions of the private rental market today.

Measuring by the number of bedrooms, people in the UK currently occupy at least twice as much housing as we need.[8] A third of us have two or more spare bedrooms, a figure that rises to 47 per cent among homeowners, while 83 per cent of homeowners have more space than they need, compared with 49 per cent for private tenants[9] and 39 per cent for social renters. The proportion having exactly the space they need is 15 per cent for owner-occupiers compared with 52 per cent for social renters.

In justifying the 'bedroom tax',[10] ministers pointed to under-occupation and low turnover in social rented homes. Social renters are much more efficient than owner-occupiers in using the space they occupy. The turnover in social renting is about 5 per cent per year: about the same as for owner-occupation, compared with 40 per cent in the private sector. The private rented sector, with short tenancies and free-market pricing, routinely reallocates housing among users, and the government finds this efficiency attractive. But if the aim of policy is to spread these benefits, then the real target must be to re-duce owner-occupation and transfer stock to private rental investors – which is in fact what we are seeing. Even so, the point where most stock is allocated through a rental market will not be reached for many decades. Meanwhile new waves of the young rely on the private rental market, where stock is limited by under-occupation and low turnover elsewhere, and prices reflect this unequally distributed supply.

Whose Benefit?

Private tenants at the lower end of the market[11] can claim Housing Benefit (HB) to pay all or part of their rent. HB is now the main way that the UK supports rented housing. It costs £25 billion per year to house about a fifth of the UK population; 36 per cent of tenants in the British private sector receive HB, rising to 71 per cent of those in the social rented sector. The average award is £108.82 per week for pri-vate tenants, £92.68 for housing association tenants and £82.38 for council tenants.[12] In the past much of this was paid directly to land-lords, but with the coming of Universal Credit (UC), tenants are start-ing to receive cash monthly in arrears and pay their own rent.

At the time of writing, UC is still being phased in, and the full results will not be seen for some time. Pilot studies[13] showed that UC did have benefits for some tenants in improved money management and cost awareness, and greater motivation to find work. But for landlords, the result was sharply increased arrears and higher costs in income recov-ery, which is always an expensive part of housing management.

What Big Teeth You Have, Grandma: The Rise (and Fall?) of Housing Associations

There are about sixteen thousand housing associations registered with the Homes and Communities Agency in England, providing over 2.6 million homes. This compares with up to 2 million private land-lords[14] owning some 5.2 million homes, often paying estate agents to manage tenancies, order repairs and collect rents.

Each housing association operates on a vastly larger scale than the great majority of private landlords but many associations are relatively small. However, around sixty associations own ten thousand homes or more. How have they got so big, when there seems to be no corresponding drive to scale-up among private landlords? One reason is development – through government grants to build or improve homes, and investment by local authorities. Another factor is VAT on running costs. Landlords can save significant amounts by 'insourcing' such things as repairs, computer systems, accounting and gas servicing – using their own directly employed staff rather than purchasing from VAT-registered contractors.

Many housing associations have developed housing-for-sale products, which are not within their charitable purposes but are held by non-charitable side-companies; some have also developed vehicles to trade freely in the private rented market.[15] The 'blended' housing association – part private, part social – is attractive if we think that the next step for private renting is to move away from the 'accidental' landlord and instead offer a more mature, professionally managed investment vehicle. Others think a fundamental clash of values may impede such 'blending'.[16]

Housing associations earn £11.6 billion per year from rents, mostly paid out of HB. They spend £5.4 billion of this on management and maintenance – about £40 per home, per week. This is big business, covering such things as repairs, rent collection, lettings and handling neighbour disputes. Large-scale ownership makes sense when it comes to borrowing, major improvements and maybe governance, but anyone looking at owner-occupation and the private sector can see that everyday repairs, lettings and rent collection are easily handled on a much smaller scale. There are potential gains in cost and quality if management and ownership are split, as has happened with council housing in the past. Such a split was the basis of a strategy for future regulation of the sector by Professor Martin Cave in 2007.[17]

Since the 1980s, government has looked to housing associations to provide its new social housing, through a mix of grant and of private finance repaid out of rents – normally met from HB. As a condition of permitting new housing, authorities require a proportion of 'social' or 'affordable' homes, so developers wanting to build homes for sale use some of the profits on other homes to subsidise the price of those earmarked for a housing association. The Coalition Government expected social landlords to charge a higher 'affordable' rent not just for the new home, but also for other homes falling vacant through turnover.

Housing associations can make a profit on their management and maintenance operations. Following the Cave review, regulation expected landlords to work with tenants to outsource these operations, and share the proceeds, but in practice this rarely happens. The profits from various sources can be packaged across a large association, or better still a group of associations, in order to build balance sheets that attract private investors. Often this has meant the loss of hard-won tenant involvement and local identity as smaller associations are merged and group structures are 'collapsed' under the control of centralised boards.

The affordable homes programme started under the Coalition Government built 170,000 homes in four years, at a cost of nearly £20 billion, of which £15 billion was raised in the money markets by large social housing groups. Raising such money to provide good homes for people with low incomes is not an achievement to be sniffed at. It requires highly skilled financial professionals answering to boards that speak their language, and complex business plans.

In July 2015, the Conservative Chancellor of the Exchequer announced a cut in rents of 1 per cent per year for three years, in order, he said, to reduce HB. In so doing, he put every housing association business plan through a shredder. It was a crude reminder of how the Treasury sees the social housing sector and the sophisticated development programme negotiated with the Coalition Government: it is one conduit through which the government procures welfare housing out of benefits paid by the Department of Work and Pensions (DWP), and it's a tap the government can turn up or down as it chooses. As a result of increased political risk, housing associations will pay more for capital. The social housing regulator had a helpful suggestion about how to prepare for that. Associations should 'consider merger'.[18]

A wider political agenda was at work.[19] On 9 September 2015, *The Times* reported:

> George Osborne has attacked housing associations for failing to deliver the homes the country needs.
>
> The 1,500 state-backed providers of affordable properties are inefficient and their performance is 'not particularly impressive', the chancellor told a House of Lords economic affairs committee as he defended the government's policy to extend right-to-buy to them.

'Is the housing association sector doing what it was designed to do, a vehicle for building homes?' he asked. 'The last data I saw, four out of five associations built no houses at all.'

This effectively classes associations as 'inactive' if they do not build homes. The business that goes with owning existing estates – managing and maintaining homes, finding and welcoming new tenants, settling neighbour disputes and building the relationships that sustain thriving neighbourhoods – is not 'activity'. Housing is understood to mean sticking things together to create more enclosures, not the economic relations that mediate the use of what is already there. This thinking views housing as 'stock' but not 'flow'.

Whether or not housing associations and councils back off from stalling the expensive right-to-buy policy, I suspect that the next Conservative manifesto will include privatising at least some associations.

In October and November 2015, the government announced a series of policy changes. 'Affordable' homes will in future be to buy rather than to rent. New social housing tenancies are to be time-limited to up to five years. A higher rate of stamp duty will apply to properties bought for private renting and private investors' relief on buy-to-let mortgages will be limited to the basic rate of tax. This shows a government moving quickly with presentational effort to address the political risks of the shift towards private renting, but the practical effect is unlikely to be more than marginal. Social housing now has little part in the policy mix.

Housing Myths

For a long time, new household formation overshot predictions as the number of single-person households grew. However, Professor Alan Holmans' analysis of the 2011 census, published in 2013,[20] reports an 'abrupt' change: fewer households than forecast, despite a higher population, compared with projections made as recently as 2008. This is partly due to more multi-generation households, maybe due to economic pressures keeping more young people with parents.

But Holmans said the 'most striking' trend was falling growth of single-person households. Approaching a million homes we had been told were 'needed' turn out not to be. And why? There are many more couple households among those aged 35+, most markedly among those aged 45 to 64. It's that pesky Please Please Me generation again, upsetting household projections by unexpectedly ceasing to live alone.

Holmans' projection assumes some return to the historic trend towards lone living, combined with the two factors that drive population growth: we are going to live longer, and we will continue to attract immigrants. But what that means for housing demand is, in truth, guesswork.

Will immigrants stay and grow families? Probably, but they might tend to form larger households. How will older people want to live? We cannot know, and previous efforts to provide for a supposedly preferred lifestyle came unstuck when we built too many small 'sheltered' flats. Demographers' terms such as 'household-forming age' become less meaningful as people enjoy their cultural and economic liberty to start later and then build a succession of households over a lifetime.

Our level of housing provision, at one home per 2.3 of population, is not low by international standards. If population rises as expected, and we want to maintain the current household size, then we will need to build 4 million homes in 20 years. At current housebuilding rates, around 120,000 per year, the average size will rise to 2.4. So do we really need more housing than is enjoyed in the USA (2.6) or Australia and New Zealand (2.7)? But if we look at Germany, with its thriving rental housing market, the ratio is 2.1. To emulate that, we need housebuilding to exceed 300,000 per year.

Meanwhile the Housing Minister promises 1 million new homes by 2020, and the drive to build new homes is combined with the political priority to protect the green belt. The result is mounting pressure on existing urban sites – most acutely, but not only, in London. Developers and large housing associations partner in programmes of 'densification.'[21] Housing associations, the 'goodies' in previous iterations of anti-clearance struggles, now find themselves fronting apparently ruthless commercial consortia in confrontation with resident groups and activists.[22] When the time comes to explain the failure to achieve 1 million homes, housing associations may be sufficiently unpopular to be a politically convenient scapegoat.

What Is To Be Done?

The housing crisis is first and foremost one of distribution. It arises from post-war welfare housing policies which determined that 'social rights' would endow generations with property rights extending through life and beyond. Now, in a sample set of ten households, three are homeowners paying nothing; another three are owners paying relatively little compared with income and property value; another three have their housing costs met partly or wholly by the state through benefit and rent regulation; and one pays the full market rent. That last one is likely to be a young worker in a middle-income bracket. Those with free or cheap housing consume more than they need. In the long transition to post-welfare housing, supply pressure is displaced especially onto market-rent payers. Their number will grow.

Devising policy to deal with this is not especially difficult. We could, for example, charge for under-occupation by counting imputed rent on land owned as taxable income. An occupancy allowance for each resident would offset the charge. Taxing imputed rent could also apply to land with planning permission. This is of course a controversial idea; but it seems to me that if the 'housing crisis' is to be properly understood and its origins and implications accepted (especially by the Please Please Me generation of debt-free homeowners) then it would be a practical way forward towards rebalancing the housing market. Some may fear that even floating such an idea is to legitimise the 'bedroom tax'. For clarification, my proposal would not affect tenants and landlords. With the 'bedroom tax', the withdrawn HB for 'spare room subsidy' applies only to poorer working-age households (not to pensioners), and to the category of consumers who are in fact the most efficient users of housing stock. It is intrinsically unfair and largely irrelevant to housing market reform.

But selling policy is a different matter, when the majority of voters have a vested interest in the current system.

We need, I think, an informed debate on two key questions.

1. **What kind of tenure do young people and other future householders want?**

The pressure group Generation Rent (GR) suggests that most want to become owner-occupiers. But that would need a return to relaxed lending conditions and, probably, prolonged house-price growth. Is that what we want? If not, what are the alternatives? I think most people would say that longer-term tenancies would enable people to plan. The private rental market, as it matures, may move in this direction. But another option is for medium-term leases (say from five to twenty years). These could be sold by the kind of 'secondary housing market' vehicle proposed by GR.[23] It could own freehold, sell leases and revalue its assets periodically; leaseholders (individuals, co-ops or landlords) could receive a premium based on revaluation.

2.   What scale of new build do we want to accommodate?

There is no certainty about what we 'need' to meet future 'demand.' Pressure to 'densify' cities threatens losing green amenity from where people need it – close to home. We could consider flexible 'modular' garden-city extensions, along the lines suggested in the winning entry to the 2014 Wolfson Economics Prize,[23] with infrastructure in place to support amenities and add housing when and if the demand is there. But as with tenure, the key to progress is an informed debate with a level of public literacy about density, cost and the real benefits of falling household size, rather than the current atmosphere of frenzy and bullying about imagined necessities.

Before any sensible discussion of our housing future can begin, the task is to speak through the noise of myth and propaganda and build an audience ready to discuss an awkward truth: our housing model has for long been unsustainable, and the upcoming generations should not be left alone to bear the cost of its failure.

Chapter 9

Homecoming

Andrew Francis

Responding to a religious leader, Jesus said, 'Foxes have holes, and birds of the air have nests; but the Son of Man has nowhere to lay his head.'[1] Popularly, this has been assumed to imply Jesus was homeless. This may well have been true, but linguistically and theologically, the saying is more likely intended to imply that during his identifiable and public ministry he had little domestic security The Greek words which Matthew records can be translated as 'Foxes have dens, birds have nests', but this is true only while these creatures are breeding, that is spreading their numbers and influence. This is exactly what Jesus was doing – the religious leader had just declared his willingness to follow Jesus wherever he went, recognising Jesus as an itinerant teacher.

Unlike foxes or birds, Jesus – the messianic 'Son of Man' – had no secure resting place. At the time of his birth, his parents were travellers, sheltering in a cattle shed, and the vulnerable trio fled from Herod's persecution to Egypt as refugees for a while. Much of Jesus' public ministry relied on the hospitality and generosity of others. He borrowed the Upper Room, and his tomb belonged to Joseph of Arimathea. There is little implication in the Gospels that Jesus owned anything beyond his robe and sandals. In the final two years of his known public ministry in Rome, the apostle Paul had little domestic security: he was under effective house-arrest in a rented home.

Life in first-century Levant was very different from life in twenty-first century Britain. For Christians, Jesus is the pivot to all theological thought, but that is always reshaped by geography and circumstance. The Bible sees believers as 'strangers in a strange land'.[2] Some years ago, theologians Stanley Hauerwas and William Willimon proposed in a book entitled *Resident Aliens*[3] that the Christian community was akin to a colony with a message, arriving on a welcoming planet. 'The message that sustains the colony is not for itself, but the whole world – the colony having significance only as God's means of saving the whole world . . . the colony is a people on the move, like Jesus' first disciples, breathlessly trying to keep up with Jesus.'[3]

Twenty-first-century Christians in Britain need a theology of housing which is Jesus-centred, rooted in biblical perspectives. This will comprise not only ideas but also practical outworking. It will not be enough simply to talk about what 'other people' or politicians ought to be doing. Surely Jesus' message about housing in Britain today will require creative stewardship, rather than increasing acquisition. It might, for some, involve increased sharing, while refining what the definition of home *should* mean for every individual and household. It may mean (as it has for several writers of this book) downsizing expectations, homes and mortgages, or letting go of property ownership. It does mean housing justice for everyone – which in turn implies accessibility, affordability and quality.

For those of my generation (now newly retired), going to Sunday school was often part of the fabric of our childhood. There we learned 'the stories of Jesus' – not just particular episodes in Jesus' own life but also some of his parables that could be clearly explained to children. The narrative of Jesus' encounter with Zacchaeus,[3] and the parables of the Prodigal Son and the Good Samaritan all were repeatedly told. All involve some form of homecoming. Jesus invited himself, and probably his itinerant band of followers, to the home of the repentant Zacchaeus, a collaborating tax collector. The errant and spendthrift Prodigal Son was richly welcomed back home by his forgiving father. The Good Samaritan left the roadside victim, whom he was helping, within the care of the innkeeper's home. Unwittingly, we were being taught a theology in which homes were places of welcome and redemption as well as security and well-being.

Personal Journeys

For all of us, our theology – our 'God-talk'[4] – is inevitably coloured by the events and experiences of our personal lives and journeys. When we try to draw together a 'theology of housing', it is helpful to be aware of our personal history. Let me offer my own as an example:

- As a student, I lived in a shared rented house. My first home away from my birth family was a flat rented from an avaricious private landlord. While training residentially for Christian ministry, my then-wife and I lived in a comfortable-but-rented seminary apartment.

- I have owned my own home, whether in a downtown neighbourhood or as a rural retreat. On several occasions, as a householder, I have had lodgers, who became friends and ultimately we became some form of proto-community, sharing meals, vehicles and regular 'quiet times' together.

- For several years, I owned a house and lived in rural SW France. I have studied in the States and worked temporarily in Scandinavia. I learned what it means to be a 'resident alien'.

- I have been a private landlord, needing to let my own distant property on occasions. At different points, I have been a trustee of three UK charities which have let residential properties to students or as 'social housing' provision. Twice during my ministry, I have served on local management boards of church-owned sheltered accommodation.

- As the son of an Anabaptist pastor, I grew up in church-owned houses, later living in several because of my own ministry around Britain. All provided as 'service tenancies', akin to club stewards or school caretakers. Now in retirement, I have been granted the lease of a house for my lifetime by the generous URC Retired Ministers' Housing Association.

I have been blessed with homes. As in the biblical narratives, I have had to learn to understand housing, and develop a theology for it, from these different perspectives. It may be helpful for you to reflect on the diversity of your lifetime's housing experience or that of your parents and children. Each of this book's contributors has used expertise gained during their professional journeys to enrich their individual viewpoints.

Hebrew Testimony

When I was a Christian minister in Leeds, a Liberal Jewish rabbi was an acquaintance of mine. He was convinced their scriptures and hymns (the Psalms) had totally begun their existence as an oral tradition. He delighted in paraphrasing the Hebrew Bible (or Old Testament) into a modern idiom. Twice, I heard him preach on Exodus 3:8: 'I will give you a home – a land flowing with milk and honey.'[5] I also heard him speak about the Hebrew prophets and the creation narratives of Genesis as rich narratives of personal liberation, all questioning what it means to live comfortably within God's creation. What is even clearer to me now than it was then is how 'God-talk' about a promised home is such a strong theme, weaving its way through the centuries, through every believer's individual life.

For our purposes, it is vital to note that:

- God is a God-of-relationship and a God who is committed to the well-being of all creation and particularly those made in the divine image: 'Male and female, [God] created them.'[6]

- To live as God intends brings blessing. Disobedience to that intention has consequences, such as Adam and Eve having to leave the security and blessing of Eden . . . yet they are not left without hope.

- God is continually redeeming and delivering people afresh, wanting them to find fresh blessing. Is this not what the Exodus story is about? Is this not why we read of the 'wilderness wanderings' so that God could give them 'a home – a land flowing with milk and honey'?

- Jewish theology and Hebrew philosophy, based on the understanding that God wanted to bring his chosen people home, underpinned the drive and struggle which brought about the modern-day state of Israel in 1948. Longing for a home is a basic human desire.

The image of a 'homeland' has become central to all the Abrahamic faiths: Judaism, Christianity and Islam. For each faith, the understanding of well-being is rooted in the development of the tribe or clan (i.e. extended family), the 'community of believers' and the peaceable caliphate respectively. As we grow increasingly to appreciate this, we realise how good theology is about specifics. Therefore our personal 'God-talk' *may* help to defuse some of the political tensions of the twenty-first century. Our theology of 'home' and housing, 'the homeland' and human well-being are all intertwined.

The concept of *shalom* (to which Chris Horton refers in Chapter 4) weaves throughout the Old Testament era into Jesus' own ministry and then forward into the life of the radical communities of disciples, down to today's generation. *Shalom* is an all-embracing sense and state of well-being, encompassing justice, wholeness, contentment, God's blessing and peace, with release from fear or violence. I have written more fully of this *shalom* understanding elsewhere.[7] *Shalom* cannot exist for individuals or communities unless all are sufficiently assured of both secure shelter and a peaceable homeland, in practical and everyday terms.

Christian Perspectives

In Sunday school, they told me Jesus was a carpenter. As I began to study Greek, I learned that really he was a *tecton*. This means Jesus was a house-builder, using carpentry skills to build a framework, out of scarce wood. Easily made mud bricks and readily available palm thatch were applied to the wooden structure to make a house. Apart from during the coldest months and days of blazing midday heat, much extended family life took place in the walled courtyards surrounding these houses in the close-packed Galilean communities of Jesus' earthly ministry. That housing pattern is still visible in the ruins of Capernaum, or on the outskirts of modern towns like Nazareth and Tiberias.

Apart from the poorest of the poor, who struggled to survive in caves or rough shelters, most first-century Christian mission was in urban communities of extended households across the Levantine Mediterranean. Jesus' own teaching ministry, and that of his accompanying itinerant supporters, relied on the households of many, for their shelter and support. Peter's home in Capernaum[8] or that of Lazarus, Martha and Mary in Bethany[9] easily spring to mind to Gospel-readers. If Peter had not received such a clear vision while enjoying hospitality of the extended Gentile household at Joppa,[10] how many dietary restrictions would Christians be living with now? Where would Paul's ministry be without the support of the extended households of many, including Lydia of Thyatira in Philippi,[11] or Aquila and Priscilla in Corinth?[12] Whether the success of Peter's fishing family, Lydia's cloth-dying or Aquila and Priscilla's tent-making businesses, Christian mission has needed the hard work of others and the willingness to share their material success, including their homes, to enable something of God's well-being for all to be revealed.

Wayne Meeks, the biblical theologian, stated about the development of Christian mission through households that these 'are essentially communal. Even those practices that are urged upon individuals in the privacy of their own homes ... are extensions of the community's practice – indeed they are means of reminding individuals even when they are alone that they are not merely devotees of the Christians' God, they are members of Christ's body, the people of God'.[13] Robert Banks' fictionalised but helpfully populist *Going to Church in the First Century*[14] emphasises such a theology. Early Christianity was a counter-culture, typified by the radical sharing of all resources.[15]

Alan and Eleanor Kreider, the Mennonite educators, are much quoted in writing that 'many outsiders find it easier to cross the threshold to a home ... than it is to enter a church building for a gathering of a Christian congregation'.[16] Houses, which are Christian homes, are again becoming essential to Christian mission. How foolish would today's Christians be to argue only for their own housing need, and not about housing needs and justice for all God's people? Otherwise once again selfish Christian advocacy becomes a stumbling block for mission.

Regrettably, I have heard too many flawed sermons upon Jesus' words in John 14: 'In my Father's house, there are many mansions.' Although Jesus goes on to say 'I go (there) to prepare a place for you', several preachers use this to limit Jesus' statement to refer only to the hereafter. Does not the phrase 'In my Father's house' have a temporal dimension, too, in that 'house' or the Greek *oikos* really means 'household', which carries both an earthly and heavenward significance? Just as much of Jesus' other teaching ties together application for rich and poor, surely Jesus' *oikos* teaching carries an understanding that there will be many different forms of homes and housing, in the here and now as well as in the life to come?

Historically, 'the monastic life remains as a testimony to share [housing], even though its forms cannot be a model for our society [generally]'.[17] Franciscan simplicity[18] and Anabaptism's 'community [sharing] of goods',[19] including housing, are well known. British examples – such as Moravian settlements (community villages),[20] Quaker garden suburbs[21] or parish alms-houses[22] – demonstrate a practical diversity in the outworking of a theology of housing. The globally acknowledged theologian, Jürgen Moltmann, wrote: 'The more we ourselves discover the oppressed, impoverished and abandoned world in our midst, the more relevant Latin American liberation theology becomes for us.'[23] One only needs to visit those who live in different neighbourhoods, rich or poor, close to us to realise that there can be a diversity of *good* housing.

The 1985 *Faith in the City* report[24] told how the church must respond to a breadth of needs, including housing, of those who are oppressed and impoverished by an increasingly divided Britain. Consequently, there is much recent theology engaging with economic practice to enable renewed patterns of biblical justice. Books such as *Liberating the Future*,[25] *For the Common Good*,[26] or my own forthcoming *OIKOS: God's Big Word for a Small Planet*,[27] exemplify this. Housing justice forms but one part of this contemporary theological exploration.

General Principles

'The sense of being lost, displaced and homeless is pervasive in contemporary culture. The yearning to belong somewhere, to have a home, to be in a safe place, is a deep and moving pursuit.'[28] God's creation of humanity and God's image in us mean that we should *not* be lost nor displaced nor homeless. We should know that we belong, and in God, we can find a security that will meet that deep, yearning, human search.

Homelessness is not what God wants for people. In medieval times, the majority of Britain's populace were only roughly housed in some form of crude shelter, which simply gave protection from the weather. Housing in the modern era has become more individual, with a lockable front door, creating material protection for goods and chattels. However, as Bishop David reminded us in Chapter 1, housing must be something more – it must have the potential to become a home, which is a place where an individual, and their kith and kin, can develop a sense of peace and increasing well-being. This does not automatically involve material acquisition or bigger houses, for it is simply the place in which people can know themselves as fully in the image of God.

When people, perhaps unaware that they are made in God's image, become 'comfortable in their own skin' and have somewhere to call 'home', they begin to 'nest' – surrounding themselves with things that enhance their sense of well-being. I have Quaker and Mennonite friends who deliberately live in comfortably furnished houses or apartments, but with fewer material possessions than their neighbours. They have created a place in which to be still, occasionally to light a candle or incense and pray, frequently gathering friends or family perhaps to share a meal, conversation, laughter and sometimes prayer. For them, a housing unit has become a home.

I need my city allotment and raised beds, where Janice (my partner) and I grow vegetables and fruit, to get 'back to the garden'; this is not essential to everyone. We might not all have the privilege of living in the Cadburys' Bournville or a garden city but in Chapter 6 Helen Woolley reminded us that quality space around our housing is vital to a 'quality of life'. Just as God promised the Hebrew people, Christians need to help create housing in our 'land flowing with milk and honey' if we are to know the blessing of God upon a whole community.

John Gummer, the former Conservative Environment Minister, often restated his personal philosophy: 'We need towns and cities where people can live, work, play and shop. We cannot continue to leave the centres to dereliction and deprivation.'[29] Such politicians are giving the church an open door to push against. A strong Christian theology of housing, which can produce a nationwide supportive network of prayerful activists who argue against self-interest, is for the good of the whole society.

There is good theology in understanding ourselves as stewards of every resource. When farming the land, on whatever scale, we quickly become aware that we are but temporary keepers of that patch of earth. The same is surely true of housing. We are *only* stewards of the property in which we live. One day, it will be handed on to another. This is true, whether you are renting it, or paying a large mortgage to build up your capital. The importance of down-sizing our wants to become consistent with our need is not just a theological challenge but a discipleship and global imperative.

A Sort of Homecoming

Several years ago, some of this book's writers contributed to a book called *Coming Home*.[30] It included a compendium of personal testimonies how, in our ways and places, we had converged in discovering a theological home within Anabaptism.[31] For us, it opened up new ways of living, prioritising life and careers as well. I named my piece 'A Sort of Homecoming'.

In the intervening years, there have been many conversations about how we should live, what our discipleship priorities are, and what 'homecoming' means. It means finding the place where our 'God-talk', our theology, can come alive in everyday bricks-and-mortar terms that affect other people's lives. The Welsh word *hiraeth* expresses that welcome and well-being as in a locus, a trusted and entrusted place.

A theology of housing needs to speak into the public square, where politicians and housing professionals alike can respond strategically. Britain needs a practical theology and a housing strategy that inform each other but also challenge the materialist philosophy that says 'bigger is better'. We need a better variety of earth-friendly housing, meeting the need of an increasingly disparate demographic. To use a Danish word, *hygge* is necessary as it implies and means 'cosy well-being'. In theological terms, that cannot apply until *all* know *hygge* in their housing.

A useful theology of housing will be coherent yet bespoke. It will recognise that 'one-size-fits-all' solutions cannot work, and will demand a set of complementary options. In the face of Britain's growing urbanisation, former Archbishop Rowan Williams stated: 'Something about the way God leads us through history, is linked, it seems, with our growth towards a situation in which we take a more and more creative role in shaping our environment.'[32] Options require creativity, and 'earth-friendly' discipleship requires wise stewardship of resources.

What matters is the recognition that every human being is uniquely made in the image of God, demanding respect, care and provision – even if that requires sacrifice or higher taxation for the rest of us. This is a theology of stewardship, of welcome and hospitality,[33] perhaps self-denial for the sake of others, knowing that our own household's example is Christian testimony in itself.

We can know when a house becomes a home, when it has become somewhere of sufficient well-being that its residents can rediscover and experience God and the nature of blessing for themselves. But for that 'homecoming' to happen, our theology must demand good and appropriate housing for every individual and family at a price that does not cost the earth – literally.

Chapter 10

A Vision for Action

Andrew Francis and Trisha Dale

People need to stop thinking of decent housing as something only a few deserve, and realise that it is something we all need. In almost all rich countries we have never had as much housing available as we have now. Never has our financial model for allocating that housing been more obviously wanting than it is now.[1]

When such an influential social commentator as Danny Dorling, whom we quoted in the Introduction, writes this in a popular book, the need for serious reflection and prophetic voices is clearly urgent.

The writers of this book have never spoken at the same conference nor even all been in the same room at the same time, yet there is a remarkable unanimity in their collected and converging voices. There is something fundamentally wrong with housing provision in Britain and there is no quick fix. The victims are not simply the homeless (although homelessness is a huge problem and worthy of its own book) but also those who are victims of an unjust system, whether as tenants or recipients of unsustainable housing loans.

In this final chapter, we have drawn together many of the broad-brush conclusions into ten action points to enable everyone, but particularly Christians, individually and as congregations or denominations, to contribute towards a new vision for housing in Britain.

1. We Are Made in God's Image

All the contributors affirm that humanity is made in God's image: 'Male and female God created them.'[2] This means there can be no division or discrimination between female and male, poor and rich, black and white, and so on. Any theology of care for God's humankind begins with unbiased provision, ensuring that welfare issues are not sidelined. Churches, in particular, need to re-engage with biblical, incarnational theology as they take the housing debate into the public square. It is a theology rooted in the principle that every person has the right to safe, secure, affordable housing for themselves and their families.

2. Housing Must Be Home-Creating, Not Investment-Driven

Too many people regard housing as an investment. This ranges from wealthy foreigners buying 'high spec' properties to domestic, small-scale, buy-to-let investors, all of whom are encouraged by current government policies. The primary purpose of housing is to enable individuals, couples, families and groups to create homes which are safe, secure, suitable and sustainable. Legislation or punitive taxation may be needed to restrict speculation or profiteering from keeping properties empty or charging exorbitant rents. Politicians especially are challenged to rethink the purpose of housing. We call for significant cross-party consideration, then legislation:

- to restrict the amount and nature of foreign or off-shore, as well as non-UK resident investment in residential property; and

- to enable the compulsory repurchase (by the local authority, for social housing) of a residential property which has been left vacant for two years or more.

3. A Call for National Consensus in Strategy and Action

The contributors appreciate the complexity of the issues involved in the creation and ongoing delivery of a just housing provision across Britain. We call for a recognition that a fresh consensus, not subject to party-political whim nor continual changes in financial priorities, is required. There was a post-war political consensus when Nye Bevan (Labour) oversaw the introduction of fresh major home-building initiatives through the 1946 and 1949 Housing Acts, which received cross-party support. In the 1950s, Harold Macmillan (Conservative) oversaw the building of nearly 300,000 homes in one calendar year. Macmillan recalled Bevan's words, 'We shall be judged in one or two years by the quantity of houses we build, but in a decade we shall be judged upon the quality of houses that we build.' We call for a similar political consensus until at least 2040 to meet Britain's housing need, creating similar stability for a generation.

That national consensus needs to include:

- a commitment to provide safe, secure, affordable and accessible housing for all;

- a recognition that we need a mix of housing provision – council housing, housing association, private rental and home-ownership; and

• an agreement to develop a rolling ten-year housing programme.

4. Affordability

A key issue in both owner-occupied and the private, social and local authority rental sectors is affordability. We believe that taxation needs to be levied upon owners who buy up high-end properties and then leave them empty to make a profit (see Point 2 above). This is particularly true in London and other large cities, effectively hyperinflating all other lower-tier property prices and rental tariffs.

We believe the government's stated 'affordable' purchase price figures (£400,000 in London and £250,000 elsewhere) are unrealistic – as well as unaffordable for the majority. Consider the salaries of such socially necessary workers as classroom teachers, ward-based health workers, transport operatives, police officers, alongside the restrictions upon lending by reputable banks or building societies. But we recognise the workers mentioned are not the lowest paid nor the poorest in society.

A just housing system will enable good, fair, rent control, facilitating tenants to afford homes and landlords properly to maintain them. We believe that the rental market requires major legislative review to ensure affordable homes but also (following the pattern of mainland European nations) to enable families and others to have long-term tenancies to help maintain educational continuity for children and community stability. Such a market needs to have a mix of provision.

5. Current National Housing Policy Must Be Recognised as Socially Divisive

One serving London councillor told us that London's housing is 'a potential tinderbox', implying that it will become a cause of social unrest, because of the current policies' innate injustices. Young Londoners do not see themselves as prospective homeowners, but most councillors already live 'on the upside of this as homeowners', and do not readily understand the gravity of the problem. Our informal sounding of contacts, including housing professionals, in other UK metropolitan areas notes similar levels of concerns about socially divisive housing policy.

We call for a commitment from each local authority to a housing plan that meets the needs of its local population, by ensuring sufficient social and council housing, a properly regulated private-rental sector and a responsible approach to mortgage lending. As writers, we note our conversations with city housing officials in both New York, USA, and Berlin, Germany, affirming these principles as central to enabling housing provision which can 'reach across' (not 'down'!) to include both migrants and the poorest-of the-poor.

We recognise that local government social welfare funding cuts mean there are fewer services for people, resulting in an increase in homelessness. This is unacceptable in modern Britain, and must be challenged. Similarly, what is termed as 'welfare reform' hits far more at the 'have nots' than the 'haves', creating further division in society. This impacts hugely on housing finance. (The issue of welfare reform is one upon which our publisher, Ekklesia, continues actively to provide commentary, analysis and policy alternatives.)

We call for a renewed debate involving all stakeholders, including tenants and the homeless, to create a less socially divisive housing strategy for Britain. However, we recognise that greater transparency is required from legislators because (as the Westminster Parliamentary Register of Interests indicates) a significant proportion of MPs have declared they are landlords of tenanted properties.

6. Accessibility and Need

The 2012 English Housing Survey found that 95 per cent of properties in England were not accessible to disabled visitors, let alone for liveability. The lack of accessible housing has been worsened by the bedroom tax and other benefit changes forcing people out of specially adapted homes they can no longer afford. While we do not believe in tokenism or unfairly categorising parts of society, we affirm that the needs of disabled, chronically ill and elderly people require formal provision.

We call for all new housing developments to be built to good access standards, and to have a proportion of fully accessible properties. We call for an abolition of the bedroom tax, and legislation that notes that disabled people require space for equipment and live-in carers. We call for an increase in funding for special needs housing to ensure sufficient development of sheltered housing, supported living, and extra-facilitated housing projects to meet a range of social care needs.

We encourage the development of *affordable* housing schemes which allow residents to move on *without penalty* as their personal circumstances require. We recognise that such accommodation must have bedroom provision for occasional/permanent carer(s) without incurring any bedroom tax. We applaud those housing providers who ensure accessibility with necessary ramps, easy access rooms and appropriate bathroom facilities. There must also be legislative protection and security of tenure for victims of illicit sub-letting.

7. Renewal of Social Housing

All the above points have implications for social housing. We believe there will always be a need for some housing to be provided by the community at large. We call for an immediate cessation of the sale of social housing. Alongside that, we argue for the building of new social housing units to increase the amount of provision. We note the past success of some city-level councils in the 'building of affordable local homes for local people'. We call upon all local authorities to invest in new social housing (at affordable rents) and challenge central government to provide match-funding.

We believe the council housing stock needs replenishing and renewing and call for a ban on the sales of local authority estates and greater restriction upon the right-to-buy policy which has taken housing out of the hands of the local community. We believe that housing associations need to be supported to maintain their original purpose of providing quality, affordable housing to help create communities.

8. Creating Turnover

The British expectation of insularity in 'a home of one's own' is not universal. We encourage the work of faith communities positively to value and demonstrate patterns of communal living. Further we encourage church-based housing schemes to create mixed-size (individual and multiple-person) housing units. We believe the implementation of more council-tax bands or possibly the introduction of land-tax banding would help to encourage more turnover in the housing market. We believe that schemes that encourage older people to share their homes with younger people will be beneficial. In addition, we would encourage incentives to help older people with larger houses to downsize, thereby releasing underused properties.

9. Open Spaces, Parks, Playgrounds and Allotments

We believe the creation and retention of maintained open spaces are vital for the quality of neighbourhoods and communities as well as the physical health and spiritual well-being of individuals. People need places to meet, and parks with adequate benches and a range of play equipment are central to this. A quarter of Britons use a park twice weekly for 'significant leisure activity'; one third of Londoners use parks regularly and one fifth of the population of the north-east visit their local park daily.[3] We advocate that voluntary organisations and churches mobilise to ensure 'Deeds of Dedication' are used to protect open spaces from either developers or local authority sale, in similar fashion to leisure gardens and allotments.

Our personal contacts with those who participate in Incredible Edible Todmorden, Bristol's food network, Cardiff's Riverside Community Allotment or Stroud's Community Agriculture co-operative lead us to affirm the need for (sub)urban vegetable-growing as providing 'open space' and being a health necessity for creating good community. There is already a legal responsibility for local authorities to provide allotments/leisure gardens 'if a need is shown to exist' (how long must a waiting list be?). Unless planning laws are sufficiently relaxed, as with Russia's dachas or Germany's Gartenschreiber, to allow temporary dwellings upon them, cultivable open space is necessary within towns and cities.

10. A Challenge to the Churches

We recognise that the majority of churchgoers are securely housed in a dwelling of their choice, as either owner-occupier or tenant. However, we call upon every congregation in Britain to engender a greater awareness of housing needs in their locality. We applaud the ecumenical initiative and challenge contained in the 'Faith in Affordable Housing' report (2009).[4] We call upon churches to act educationally, ecumenically and strategically in developing better regional housing policies. We call upon churches to support grass-roots campaigns in their community. Further, we invite every British congregation to review the use of their premises in helping meeting the needs of both homeless and 'housing victims' since the 1985 publication and recommendations of *Faith in the City*. Then we invite those congregations to improve upon that review in study, prayer and action.

This book is subtitled 'Christian Reflections upon Britain's Housing Need'. It is but one contribution to a necessary debate which must take place in every community, on every tier of government and for every form of housing provider. We recognise that our unwritten subtext has been about the quality and nature of 'community' – from neighbourhood to city level – but this book is about housing and cannot attempt resolve any other issues of community-building.

The contributors are all followers of Jesus of Nazareth. This 'Son of Man with nowhere to lay his head' was born in a borrowed stable, survived as a refugee child and lay dead in a borrowed tomb. Yet Jesus came that the world might have life in all its fullness and, until all those who suffer under an unjust housing system are victims no longer, Jesus' followers today still have much prayerful restorative action to undertake.

Resources

National Organisations

Defend Council Housing – Campaign group working against depletion of council housing across England, Scotland and Wales. http://www. defendcouncilhousing.org.uk/dch/

Generation Rent – Works for professionally managed, secure, decent and affordable housing. http://www.generationrent.org/

Homes for Britain – Calls for affordable housing across the UK. http:// homesforbritain.org.uk/

Homes for Wales – Campaign group for affordable housing in Wales. http://homesfor.wales/

Housing Justice – The national Christian voice on housing and homelessness. Provides advice and training for groups working with homeless people in their community and campaigns for just housing policies. Also leads the Faith in Affordable Housing programme (http:// www.housingjustice.org.uk/pages/fiah.html) that enables churches to release buildings to their local community for affordable housing. http:// www.housingjustice.org.uk/

Housing Options Scotland – Help for disabled people, older people and veterans. http://www.housingoptionsscotland.org.uk

Housing Rights Information – Support for migrants and new arrivals in Scotland. http://www.housing-rights.info/scotland/index.php

Housing Scotland Today – The national representative body for Scotland's housing associations and co-operatives. http://www. housingscotlandtoday.com

Living Rent – Campaigns for fair rents for people living in private rental accommodation in Scotland. http://www.livingrent.org/

National Housing Federation – National body of housing associations in England. http://www.housing.org.uk/

Positive Action in Housing – Provides advice and information to immigrants and refugees in Scotland. http://www.paih.org/

Poverty Truth Commission – Brings together decision makers and people living at the sharp end in housing and other areas. Scottish initiative, spreading to England. http://www.faithincommunityscotland. org/poverty-truth-commission/

Priced Out – Project focusing on affordable housing. http://www. pricedout.org.uk/

Shelter (England) – The national campaign on issues relating to housing and homelessness in England and Scotland. http://www.shelter.org.uk/

Shelter Cymru – Partner organisation which campaigns in Wales. http:// sheltercymru.org.uk/

Shelter Scotland – tackling housing and homelessness in Scotland. http://scotland.shelter.org.uk

Shout (Social Housing Under Threat) – Calls for investment in social housing. http://www.4socialhousing.co.uk/

Local Groups

Aylesbury Tenants First – Southwark-based campaign protesting against sell-off of Aylesbury Estate. http://aylesburytenantsfirst.org.uk/

Focus E15 Mothers – Newham-based campaign group that began by single mothers resisting the closure of the hostel where they lived and which has developed to campaign against the sell-off of local council housing and a commitment to local housing for local people. http:// focuse15.org/

Save Cressingham Gardens – Lambeth-based campaign group that is working to save the Cressingham Gardens estate from being sold off. https://savecressingham.wordpress.com/

Sweets Way Resists – Barnet-based campaign group resisting sale of Sweets Way. https://sweetswayresists.wordpress.com/

Welsh Streets – Liverpool group working to repair rather than demolish homes. http://www.welshstreets.co.uk/

Contributors

Andrew Francis is a community theologian, published poet, environmentalist and retired URC minister. His theological books include *Anabaptism: Radical Christianity* (2010), *Hospitality and Community After Christendom* (2012), *What in God's Name Are You Eating?* (2014), *Shalom: the Jesus Manifesto (2016)* and his forthcoming *OIKOS: God's Big Word for a Small Planet* on economy, ecology and ecumeny. A keen allotmenteer, baker, jam-maker and joyful cook, he lives in Wiltshire.

Trisha Dale has been involved with the Anabaptist Network since its earliest days. She is an experienced editor of books and academic journals, and worked on most of the 'After Christendom' series published by Paternoster, now living in Birmingham.

Sean Gardiner joined the Mennonites and the Labour Party in 1984. He is Financial Inclusion Manager for Homes for Haringey. From 1989 to 2013 he managed the housing team on the Broadwater Farm estate in Tottenham. He lives in Tower Hamlets on the thirteenth floor, with his wife, Judith, and has two children, both working for voluntary organisations.

Chris Horton is a solicitor with master's degrees in both law and theology, who splits working time between Wrekin Housing Trust, as company secretary, and All Nations, Wolverhampton, a multi-ethnic Assemblies of God church where he is an elder. Married, with three grown-up children, he is passionate about family, hill-walking and cross-cultural mission.

Paul Lusk was a prizewinning politics scholar at Oxford University and has spent almost forty years in housing, developing co-operatives and other resident-controlled solutions for new building, regeneration and neighbourhood management. He is a Baptist belonging to an independent church..

Helen Roe, AA Dipl RIBA ARB, is a partner in north London architects, Atkinson Roe Architects and Designers. Helen is passionate about sustainability and making cities great places to be. Her work includes commercial interiors, and educational and community projects. A member of the United Reformed Church, she enjoys worshipping with all denominations. She met Andrew Francis when they were both trustees of the London Mennonite Trust.

The Right Reverend Doctor *David Walker* has served as a volunteer governor in the field of housing and homelessness since the mid-1980s. As well as chairing a number of housing associations and secular charities he was the first chair of the Christian organisation, Housing Justice, and is a former chair of the Housing Committee of the Church of England Pensions Board. After 17 years in parochial ministry, he served as Bishop of Dudley from 2000 to 2013. David is now Bishop of Manchester, a return to the area he grew up in, and a Church Commissioner. In 2014 he gained his PhD for his researches into the nature of Christian belonging.

Helen Woolley is a chartered landscape architect and Reader in Landscape Architecture and Society in the Department of Landscape at the University of Sheffield. Her research and knowledge exchange activities have two strands – green and open space, and children and young people's outdoor environments – and has been funded by government departments, research councils, non-governmental organisations, charities and private companies. Building on research about children's outdoor environments in post disaster north-east Japan, Helen is currently exploring issues about children's outdoor environments in high-density cities and in crisis situations.

Raymond Young has been involved in housing in Scotland for over forty years professionally with the Housing Corporation and Scottish Homes, including rural-housing policy development. For ten years he chaired Rural Housing Service. He lives in rural Perthshire and is a member of the Iona Community.

Financial Supporters

Foxes Have Holes has been made possible thanks to generous support from the following people on Indigogo, plus a number of others who chose to remain anonymous. We are grateful to each and every one of you for your support:

Chris Allen
Janet Archer
Neil Barton
Robert Bryce
Janet Bunker
Dr Kit Byatt
E.A. Drake
John Duffy
John Farrar
R. Gillingham
Liz Griffiths
Janice Heath
Graham Marshall
Michael Marten

Simon Meadows
Lucy Moffat
Nick Money
Peter O'Connell
Simon Oxley
Richard Peat
Michael Powis
Lee Reddyhoff
Revd Julian Templeton
Iorwerth Owain Thomas
Dr J.H. Thompson
Stephen R. Ward
Nicholas Wood
Rachel Yule

About Ekklesia

Ekklesia is an independent, not-for-profit think-tank which orients its work around the changing role of beliefs, values and faith or non-faith in public life.

We advocate transformative ideas and solutions to societal challenges based on a strong commitment to social justice, non- violence, environmental responsibility, nonconformist styles of Christianity, and a creative exchange among those of different convictions (religious and otherwise).

Ekklesia is committed to promoting – alongside others – new models of mutual economy, conflict transformation, social power, restorative justice, community engagement and political participation.

We are also working to encourage alternative perspectives on humanitarian challenges in a globalised world, not least a positive, affirming approach to migration.

Overall, we are concerned both with the policy, practice and theology of moving beyond a top-down 'church of power', and with challenging top-down, unjust models of economy and politics in society as a whole.

This means that, while we are a Christian political think-tank rooted in Anabaptist values, we are happy to work with people of many backgrounds, both 'religious' and 'non-religious', who share common values and approaches.

Ekklesia's reports, analysis and commentary can be accessed via our website here: www.ekklesia.co.uk

Acknowledgements

There are many people who have influenced, as well as created, this book. First, I need to thank the chapter contributors, for their wise insights and professional skills: Sean Gardiner, Chris Horton, Paul Lusk, Helen Roe, Bishop David Walker, Helen Woolley and Raymond Young. I am grateful to Alison Gelder, of Housing Justice, for her Foreword, and all those who have given such positive comments, published here.

I owe much gratitude to Trisha Dale, a long-time friend and professional editor, for her work with me in the Introduction and final chapter, as well as encouraging the voices of our co-writers to be heard.

Thank you to Ekklesia, the Christian think-tank, for having the courage and taking the risk to publish this timely book. Personally, I am grateful to them for the robust support of Simon Barrow (Co-Director) and Virginia Moffatt (Chief Operating Officer).

I remain grateful to Martin Atkinson, for the cover photograph, and to the Hodby Studio for the cover design concept. Thanks to Bob Carling for the speedy production.

Finally, thank you for reading this – may God bless your activism and prayer. Omissions and mistakes are finally down to me. But without the unflinching support of Janice, my partner, this book would have never got this far.

A note about the front cover

The front-cover photograph shows a section of 'container city' – a masterpiece of inexpensive urban housing, conceived by Eric Reynolds of Urban Space Management. Helen Roe tells the story more fully, in Chapter 5. One does not need to be an architect to appreciate Reynolds' lateral thinking; I have known and enjoyed his work for nearly two decades.

The use of discarded containers – so much a symbol of our international lives and consumerism – to provide inexpensive housing alternatives is a creative upcycling of apparently 'scrap' material to meet part of Britain's housing need. Reynolds' container city is but one of many solutions that we need to find. These slabs of urban colour are reminiscent of Mondrian's artistic style.

Piet Mondrian (1872–1944) was a Dutch painter and co-founder of the *De Stijl* movement with Theo van Doesberg. Mondrian's middle years' work, of rectilinear gatherings of primary colours and white divided by clean black lines, became the inspiration for this book's cover. Since Mondrian's death, this style has been reproduced in furnishings, textiles and household goods as well as in building design. Such modernist Mondrian-inspired murals can be found across Britain from the poverty of areas of Sunderland or urban Yorkshire to areas of metropolitan gentrification. Colour and design, such as Mondrian's or Reynolds', remind us of the importance of creativity as we seek to fulfil Britain's housing need.

Andrew Francis

Endnotes

Introduction

1   Danny Dorling, *All That Is Solid: How the Great Housing Disaster Defines Our Times and What We Can Do About It?* (London, UK: Penguin, 2014).

2   www.independent.co.uk/ (25 Jan. 2016).

Chapter 2

1   Andy Wightman, *The Poor Had No Lawyers: Who Own Scotland (and How They Got It)* (Edinburgh, UK: Birlinn, 2015).

2   Brian Inglis, *Poverty and the Industrial Revolution* (London, UK: Panther/Granada, 1972), p. 107.

3   E.P. Thomson, *The Making of the English Working Class* (London, UK: Penguin, 1968), p. 352.

4   Alistair Moffatt, *The Reivers: The Story of the Border Reivers* (Edinburgh: Birlinn, 2008).

5   Until 1991, more Scots rented than owned the property in which they lived. The 2011 UK Census indicated that it was still just about 62 per cent compared with over 80per cent for England.

6   Lesley Riddoch, *Blossom: What Scotland Needs to Flourish* (Edinburgh, UK: Luath Press, 2013), p. 65.

7   *Glasgow Herald* figures.

8   Raymond Young, *Annie's Loo: The Govan Origins of Scotland's Community-Based Housing Organisations* (Argyll, UK: Argyll, 2013).

9   Maurice Beresford, 'The Face of Leeds, 1780–1914', in *The History of Modern Leeds* (ed. Derek Fraser; Manchester, UK: Manchester University Press, 1980), p. 98.

10   Ebenezer Howard, *Garden Cities of Tomorrow* (Eastbourne, UK: Attic Books, 1985).

11   Howard, *Garden Cities*, p. 105.

12   John D. Beasley, *The Story of Peckham* (London, UK: London Borough of Southwark, 1976).

13   Nicholas Bullock, *Building the Post-War World* (London, UK: Routledge, 2002).

14   Hazel Evans (ed.), *New Towns: The British Experience* (London, UK: Charles Knight, 1972); Lynsey Hanley, *Estates: An Intimate History* (London: Granta Books, 2012).

15 Riddoch, *Blossom*, p. 128.
16 Michael Harloe, *Swindon: A Town in Transition* (London, UK: Heinemann, 1975).
17 Patrick Abercrombie, *Greater London Plan* (London, UK: HMSO, 1945).
18 Peter Ackroyd, *London – The Biography* (London, UK: Vintage, 2001), p. 759.
19 David Smith, *Something Will Turn Up: Britain's Economy, Past, Present and Future* (London, UK: Profile, 2015), p. 35.
20 Andrew Rigby, *Communes in Britain* (London, UK: Routledge & Kegan Paul, 1974), pp. 40–67.
21 Clem Gorman, *People Together* (St. Albans, UK: Paladin, 1975), p. 65.
22 Andy Worthington, *The Battle of the Beanfield* (Eyemouth, UK: Enabler Publications, 2005).
23 HRH Charles, Prince of Wales, *A Vision of Britain: A Personal View of Architecture* (London, UK: Doubleday, 1989).
24 ACUPA, *Faith in the City: A Call for Action by Church and Nation* (London: UK: Church House, 1985).
25 David Pepper, *Communes and the Green Vision* (London, UK: Green Print/Merlin Press, 1991).
26 Ackroyd, *London*, p. 604.
27 *Sunday Times Magazine* (1 Nov. 2015), p. 22.
28 As reported on 25 July 2015, on BBC Radio 4, as well as in *The Times* and *The Independent*.
29 As reported on 16 January 2016 by BBC on Radio 4 and other news bulletins as well as in *The Guardian, The Times* and *The Independent*.
30 John Gringrod, *Concretopia: A Journey Around the Rebuilding of Postwar Britain* (London, UK: Old Street Publishing, 2013).

Chapter 3

David Sheppard, *Bias to the Poor* (London: Hodder & Stoughton, 1983).

1 Judith Gardiner, 'Getting Stuck in: Anabaptist Involvement in Local Politics', in *At Peace and Unafraid* (Duane K. Friesen and Gerald Schlabach, eds; Harrisonburg, VA, USA: Herald Press, 2005), p. 368.
2 Alison Ravetz, *Council Housing and Culture* (London: Routledge, 2001), p. 78.
3 David Hall, *Working Lives* (London: Bantam Press, 2012), p. 22.

4   Laurie Green, *Blessed are the Poor?* (London: SCM Press, 2015), p. 50.

5   Hall, *Working Lives*, p. 26.

Chapter 4

1   Andrew Arden, *Manual of Housing Law* (London: Sweet & Maxwell, 1983), p. 3. Andrew Arden is widely regarded as the pre-eminent lawyer in the field though others are following in the path he pioneered.

2   In October 2015, the Office for National Statistics decided that housing associations are public bodies due to the statutory controls imposed in the Housing and Regeneration Act 2008, which put onto statutory footing some of the controls the housing regulator had previously exercised through persuasion. At the time of writing the government is considering legislative changes to lessen the control on mergers and disposals of properties so that the estimated £60 billion debt of registered proprietors does not count as public-sector debt.

3   The numbers owned or managed can change rapidly due to mergers. For recent statistics on those associations that have developed new units, see http://m.insidehousing.co.uk/the-tipping-point/7010136, accessed 17 September 2015.

4   The Homes and Communities Agency, as regulator, maintains the register of providers of social housing. Some of the registered providers are not truly recognisable as housing associations. https://www.gov.uk/government/publications/current-registered-providers-of-social-housing

5   Peter Malpass, *Housing Associations and Housing Policy: A Historical Perspective* (Basingstoke: Macmillan, 2000), p. 177.

6   Malpass, *Housing Associations*, p. 178.

7   James Tickell, *Turning Hopes into Homes: A History of Social Housing 1235–1996* (London: National Housing Federation, 1996).

8   Malpass, *Housing Associations*, p. 30.

9   W. Jordan, *Philanthropy in England 1480–1660* (London: Allen & Unwin, 1959), p. 153

10 Malpass, *Housing Associations*, p. 32.

11 Malpass, *Housing Associations*, p. 32.

12 This is an extract from the deed constituting the Bournville Village Trust. P. Henslowe, *Ninety Years On: An Account of the Bournville Village Trust* (Bournville: Bournville Village Trust, 1984).

13 O. Hill, 'Cottage Property in London', *Fortnightly Review* (November 1866), reprinted in O. Hill, *The Homes of the London Poor* (Cambridge: Cambridge University Press, 2010), p. 19.

14 Malpass, *Housing Associations*, p. 33.

15 Malpass, *Housing Associations*, p. 37.

16 Malpass, *Housing Associations*, p. 69.

17 Malpass, *Housing Associations*, p. 79.

18 Samuel Jones, ed., *The Enduring Relevance of Octavia Hill* (London: Demos, 2012), *passim.*

19 Malpass, *Housing Associations*, p. 142. For example, the British Churches Housing Association was set up in 1964 to promote formation of housing associations around the country and the Catholic Housing Aid Society predated it by ten years but was likewise particularly active from the mid-1960s.

20 Malpass, *Housing Associations*, p. 177.

21 The Act consolidated and reformed the existing legislation and introduced a greater emphasis on tenants as consumers or customers entitled to involvement and good quality services. However the policy aim of promoting home ownership remained paramount.

22 *Housing* (London: HMSO, 1987).

23 Malpass, *Housing Associations*, p. 252.

24 http://www.lgcplus.com/shaftesbury-housing-association-among-worst-performing/1251191.article, accessed 15 September 2015.

25 http://m.insidehousing.co.uk/no-star-double-shows-slow-progress-for-shaftesbury/1446711.article. http://www.theguardian.com/society/2005/sep/01/communities, accessed 15 September 2015.

26 Matthew 5:14, ESV.

27 The principle of decay or winding down will be reversed, at least on my reading of Romans 8:20–25, when the people of God come to a maturity that demonstrates the life of the kingdom and releases the fullness of the new creation. The focus of this chapter, however, is on housing associations rather than eschatology!

28 Malpass, *Housing Associations*, p. 212. This might seem to be self-evident from a cursory review of the National Housing Federation website or the pages of *Inside Housing*, a weekly news magazine focused on the social housing sector. See also Michael E. Stone, *Social Housing in the UK and US: Evolution, Issues and Prospects* (London: Goldsmiths College, 2003), p. 17.

Chapter 5

1   Forest Research case study, Regeneration of previously developed land 028 Olympic Park http://forestry.gov.uk/website/searchall.nsf/ SearchTemplate?OpenForm&Country=gb;Areas=General%20 Information:News%20Releases:Publications:Public%20Register%20 of%20planting%20and%20felling%20applications:Forest%20 Research;query=%22olympic%20park%22

2   http://www.queenelizabetholympicpark.co.uk/our-story/the-legacy-corporation/business-plan
London Legacy Development Corporation ten year plan 2015/2016 to 2024/2025 Approved by LLDC Board 17 March 2015.

3   http://www.queenelizabetholympicpark.co.uk/our-story/the-legacy-corporation/business-plan '3. Objectives – what we will do in 10 years', p. 8.

4   www.queenelizabetholympicpark.co.uk Olympic legacy Supplementary Planning Guidance July 2012.pdf

5   www.urbanspace.com Trinitybuoywharf.com

6   http://www.telegraph.co.uk/finance/property/3300326/Reynolds-law. html

7   http://www.hackney.gov.uk/Assets/Documents/review_of_live-work_policy_in_hackney_-_london_residential_research.pdf

8   http://uli.org/case-study/uli-case-study-kings-cross-london-united-kingdom/

9   download from https://www.google.co.uk/search?client=safari& rls=en&q=www.argent+principles+for+a+human+city&ie=UTF-8&oe=UTF-8&gfe_rd=cr&ei=IdtvVuCHN6Xj8wevqp24Bg&g ws_rd=ssl

10   www.kingscross.co.uk / development

11   https://www.london.gov.uk/what-we-do/planning/london-plan/ current-london-plan/london-plan-chapter-3/policy-33-increasing

12   https://www.london.gov.uk/what-we-do/planning/implementing-london-plan/opportunity-areas
https://www.london.gov.uk/what-we-do/planning/implementing-london-plan/supplementary-planning-guidance/housing-supplementary

13   http://michaeledwards.org.uk/wp-content/uploads/2015/04/KXC-s106-Variation-LBC-Officers-report.pdf

Chapter 6

1   A.G. Gardiner, *Life of George Cadbury* (London: Cassell, 1923).

2   Bournville Village Trust, *Landscape and Housing Development* (London: B.T. Batsford, 1949), p. 32.

3   Bournville Village Trust, *Landscape and Housing Development*.

4   Gardiner, *Life of George Cadbury*.

5   Bournville Village Trust, *When We Build Again: A Study Based on Research into Conditions of Living and Working in Birmingham* (London: George Allen & Unwin, 1941).

6   Bournville Village Trust, *When We Build Again*, p. 83.

7   V. Hole, *National Building Studies Research Paper 39: Children's Play on Housing Estates* (London: Her Majesty's Stationery Office, 1966); Department of the Environment, *Children at Play* (London: Her Majesty's Stationery Office, 1973).

8   R. Wheway and A. Millward, *Child's Play: Facilitating Play on Housing Estates* (Coventry: Chartered Institute of Housing with support from the Joseph Rowntree Foundation, 1977).

9   C. Allen, M. Camina, T. Casey, S. Coward and M. Wood, *Mixed Tenure Twenty Years on: Nothing out of the Ordinary* (Coventry, UK: Chartered Institute of Housing for the Joseph Rowntree Foundation, 2005); J. Horton, P. Christensen, P. Kraftl and S Hadfield Hill, 'Walking . . . Just Walking: How Children and Young People's Everyday Pedestrian Practices Matter', *Social and Cultural Geography* 15(1), 2014, pp. 94–115.

10 Sugiyama, T., C. Ward Thompson and S. Alves, 'Associations between neighbourhood open space attributes and quality of life for older people in Britain', *Environment and Behavior* 41, (2009), pp. 3–21.

11 H. Woolley, *Urban Open Spaces* (London: Routledge, 2003).

12 H. Thorpe, E. Galloway and L Evans, *From Allotments to Leisure Gardens: A Case Study of Birmingham*. (Birmingham: Leisure Gardens Research Unit, University of Birmingham, 1976).

13 H. Thorpe, *The Report of the Department Committee of Inquiry into Allotments* (London: Her Majesty's Stationery Office, 1969).

14 www.nsalg.org.uk/allotment-info/brief-history-of-allotments (last accessed 3 March 2016).

15 www.incredible-edible-todmorden.co.uk (last accessed 13 October 2015).

16 Woolley, *Urban Open Spaces*.

Chapter 7

1   M. Shucksmith, *Scotland's Rural Housing: A Forgotten Problem*

(Perth: Rural Forum, 1984).

2 See www.gov.scot/Topics/Statistics/About/Methodology/UrbanRu-ralClassification

3 Rural Policy Centre, *Rural Scotland in Focus* (Edinburgh: SAC, 2014).

4 J. Hunter, *From the Low Tide of the Sea to the Highest Mountain Tops: Community Ownership of Land in the Highlands and Islands of Scotland* (Is of Lewis: Carnegie UK / Islands Book Trust, 2012).

5 A fuller account of rural housing association development is in R. Young, *Affordable Homes in Rural Scotland: The Role of Housing Associations* (Edinburgh: Capercaille, 2015).

6 The story of community-based housing associations is told in R. Young, *Annie's Loo: The Govan Origins of Scotland's Community Based Housing Associations* (Glendaruel: Argyll).

7 Hunter, *From the Low Tide of the Sea.*

8 Land Reform Review Group Final Report, *The Land of Scotland and the Common Good* (Edinburgh: Scottish Government, 2014).

9 Rural Affairs and Environment Committee, *5th Report, 2009 (Session 3) Rural Housing* (Edinburgh: Scottish Parliament, 2009).

10 OECD, *Rural Policy Reviews: Scotland, UK* (Paris: OECD, 2009).

11 D. Alexander, *Rural Housing Burdens: How Effective Have They Been?* (Dunfermline: Carnegie UK, 2011).

12 Energy Advisory Service, *Fuel Poverty Report 2014* (Edinburgh: TEAS / Comhairle nan Eilean Siar, 2014).

13 Planning Advice Note 2/2010 – *Affordable Housing and Housing Land Audits, Scottish Government* (Edinburgh, 2010).

Chapter 8

1 House prices are from the Nationwide house price index. As only a fraction of homes are sold in any one period, the actual average transaction cost is adjusted in any index to provide a 'typical' figure. For a fuller study of indexing, see Acadata, 'Which Houseprice Index?' (July 2014).

2 It is often said that housebuilding programmes were much larger in the past, which is true. But the large-scale, public-sector house-building of the mid-twentieth century was part of huge 'slum clearance' programmes, so the actual net stock growth was much less than the scale of building. UK's housing stock relative to population has grown fairly steadily.

3 T.H. Marshall, *Citizenship and Social Class* (Cambridge: Cambridge

University Press, 1950).

4   'The Impact of Interest Rates on the Household Sector', in the Bank of England quarterly bulletin, Q4 2014 http://www.bankofengland. co.uk/publications/Documents/quarterlybulletin/2014/qb14q405.pdf

5   http://www.bankofengland.co.uk/financialstability/Pages/fpc/intereststress.aspx

6   http://www.theguardian.com/business/2014/jun/26/bank-of-england-limit-large-loans-housebuyers-mortgage-lenders

7   Social housing is likely to move towards fixed-term tenancies in accordance with Coalition legislation.

8   These figures are from the 2011 UK census accessed through NOMIS tables for England and Wales.

9   The dataset used here includes small numbers of rent-free and old 'fair rent' regulated tenancies.

10 Officially known as the 'spare room subsidy', this restricts the amount of housing benefit paid to tenants who 'under-occupy' social housing. This currently affects about 450,000 tenants who lose an average of £15.24 per week, which they need to find by other means such as saving on other expenditure or sub-letting a room. The 'bedroom tax' was introduced by the Coalition Government and brought social housing into line with the system already applying in the private rented sector.

11 The ceiling for private sector HB is set by the Local Housing Allowance representing the lower end of the rental market in each area. For details and local rates see https://www.gov.uk/government/publications/understanding-local-housing-allowances-rates-broad-rental-market-areas

12 HB caseload statistics for Great Britain, May 2015.

13 DWP, *Direct Payment Demonstration Projects: Key Findings of the Programme Evaluation* (December 2014).

14 *Daily Telegraph* (22 October 2014).

15 For example, Fizzy Living, a subsidiary of Thames Valley Housing Association, specialises in rented housing for young professionals.

16 For an interesting insight into this debate from a private-sector perspective, see on the Royal Institute of Chartered Surveyors website: www.rics.org/uk/news/news-insight/comment/social-ambitions-the-risks-facing-housing-associations-moving-into-the-prs/#

17 Martin Cave, *Every Tenant Matters: A Review of Social Housing Regulation* (Wetherby, CLG Publications, June 2007). Cave's

analysis ignored VAT.

18 http://www.socialhousing.co.uk/rps-should-consider-merger-
    if-necessary-and-be-ready-for-higher-cost-of-debt-says-
    regulator/7011835.article (18 September 2015).

19 Alan Holmans, *New Estimates of Housing Demand and Need in
    England, 2011 to 2031*, (Town and Country Planning Association,
    2013).

20 'Home Truths', London First (1 March 2014) http://londonfirst.co.uk/
    wp-content/uploads/2014/03/LF_HOUSING_REPORT.pdf

21 http://www.oceanmediagroup.co.uk/features/housingprotests/

22 In its 2015 'Queens speech': http://www.generationrent.org/
    demand_a_queens_speech_on_housing

23 http://www.policyexchange.org.uk/images/
    WolfsonPrize2014/20140827%20rudlin%20stage%202.pdf

Chapter 9

1   Matthew 8:20, NRSV.

2   See Exodus 2:22; 1 Peter 2:11.

3   Stanley Hauerwas and William Willimon, *Resident Aliens* (Nashville,
    TN: Abingdon Press, 1989), p. 51.

4   Andrew Francis, *Shalom: The Jesus Manifesto* (Milton Keynes, UK:
    Paternoster, 2016), 'Introduction'.

5   Author's paraphrase.

6   Genesis 1:27, NRSV; see Matthew 19:4.

7   Francis, *Shalom*, chapter 2.

8   Matthew 8.

9   John 11.

10 Acts 10.

11 Acts 16.

12 Acts 18.

13 Wayne Meeks, *Origins of Christian Morality* (Yale, MA: Yale
    University Press, 1995), p. 110.

14 Robert Banks, *Going to Church in the First Century* (Beaumont, TX:
    Seedsowers Christian Publishing House, 1980).

15 Acts 2.

16 Alan Kreider and Eleanor Kreider, *Worship and Mission after
    Christendom* (Milton Keynes, UK: Paternoster, 2010), p. 215.

17 Ian Adams, *Cave – Refectory – Road*, publisher's back-cover
    comment (Norwich, UK: Canterbury Press, 2010).

18 Brother Ramon, *Franciscan Simplicity: Following St. Francis Today*

(London, UK: SPCK, 2nd edn, 2008).

19 James Stayer, *The German Peasants' War and Anabaptist Community of Goods* (Montreal, Quebec: McGill-Queen's University Press, 1994).

20 Ron Southern, *In His Arms: Life in an English Moravian Settlement in the Eighteenth Century* (UK: Lulu.com, 2011).

21 See Chapters 2 and 6.

22 W.H. Godfrey, *The English Almshouse* (London, UK: Faber & Faber, 1955).

23 Jürgen Moltmann, 'Political Theology and Theology of Liberation', in *Liberating the Future: God, Mammon and Theology* (ed. Joerg Rieger; Minneapolis, MN: Augsberg Fortress, 1998), p. 78.

24 *Faith in the City: The Report of the Archbishop of Canterbury's Commission on Urban Priority Areas* (Church House Publishing, 1985).

25 Moltmann, 'Political Theology', p. 78.

26 Herman E. Daly and John B. Cobb Jnr, *For the Common Good* (New York, NY: Beacon Press, 1994).

27 Andrew Francis, *OIKOS: God's Big Word for a Small Planet* (Eugene, OR: Cascade, forthcoming).

28 Walter Brueggemann, *The Land* (Minneapolis, MN: Fortress Press, 2nd edn, 2002), p. 1.

29 John Gummer, 'Those Four Million Homes', in *Town and Country* (ed. Anthony Barnett and Roger Scruton; London, UK: Jonathan Cape, 1998).

30 Alan Kreider and Stuart Murray, eds., *Coming Home: Stories of Anabaptists in Great Britain and Ireland* (Kitchener, Ont.: Pandora Press, 2000).

31 Andrew Francis, *Anabaptism: Radical Christianity* (Bristol, UK: Antioch Papers, 2010).

32 Rowan Williams, 'Urbanisation, the Christian Church and the Human Project', in *Spirituality in the City* (ed. Andrew Walker; London, UK: SPCK, 2005), p. 15.

33 Andrew Francis, *Hospitality and Community after Christendom* (Milton Keynes, UK: Paternoster, 2012).

Chapter 10

1 Danny Dorling, *All That Is Solid: How the Great Housing Disaster Defines Our Times and What We Can Do About It?* (London, UK: Penguin, 2014), p. 302.

2   See Genesis 1:27.
3   2015 survey figures from the Fields in Trust charity.
4   www.fiah.org.uk

Housing Justice

Housing Justice was created in 2003 when CHAS (Catholic Housing Aid Society) and CNHC (Churches' National Housing Coalition) merged. In January 2006 Housing Justice expanded further when it merged with UNLEASH (Church Action on Homelessness in London).

Housing Justice combines over 60 years' experience with the energy of a fresh organisation. We enable local groups and churches to provide practical help to people in housing need. At the same time we work for change in housing policies at national and local level. We do this by embracing partnership with people of all faiths (and none) who share our values of social justice and compassion.

At the Housing Justice launch, participants added their signatures to a banner outside the church demanding Decent Housing and calling for every person to have a home that truly meets their needs.

Cardinal Cormac Murphy-O'Connor, speaking at the launch, said:

> To have somewhere we call home is a fundamental part of our human dignity. Home is the place where we build our families and find the space to develop alongside friends and loved ones. To be deprived of such a basic necessity is to feel less than human.
>
> A just society must care for all its members, but especially those in most need. As Christians and Catholics we have a special responsibility to work on behalf of homeless people. We must be their advocates, and we must do everything we can to provide for their needs, both practical and spiritual.

Housing Justice: http://www.housingjustice.org.uk

The Iona Community is a dispersed ecumenical Christian community which was founded in 1938 by George MacLeod, then a Church of Scotland parish minister in Govan, Glasgow. George brought together young ministers in training and unemployed craft workers to rebuild the ancient monastic buildings of the Benedictine Abbey which had lain in ruins since the Reformation. Through this common task they discovered a common life together.

The Iona Community, therefore, was born as a practical response to the needs of people struggling with the challenges of poverty, poor housing and unemployment in 1930s Glasgow. And out of the perception that the Church no longer spoke to the reality of their lives.

Ever since, the commitment to economic justice and the inclusion of the poorest and most vulnerable in society have been central to the Iona Community's life and work. Today this is expressed in many ways: through engagement with poor communities throughout Britain and across the world, in advocacy for justice and peace, in support for refugees and asylum-seekers and in working with marginalised young people on the mainland and in our island centres.

More about the Iona Community: http://iona.org.uk

Lightning Source UK Ltd.
Milton Keynes UK
UKOW02f0402140416

272209UK00001B/56/P